Key Stage 3

Englisn

Ages 13–14

Steve Foster and Judith Polley

survival GUIDE

To the many pupils I have enjoyed teaching.
Judith Polley

Acknowledgements

The authors and publisher are grateful to the copyright holders, as credited, for permission to use quoted materials and photographs.

Cider with Rosie by Laurie Lee, published by Hogarth Press. Reprinted by permission of The Random House Group Ltd.

Every effort has been made to trace the copyright holders and to obtain their permission for the use of copyright material. The author and publisher will gladly receive information enabling them to rectify any error or omission in subsequent editions.

Letts Educational
Chiswick Centre
414 Chiswick High Road
London W4 5TF
Tel: 020 8996 3333
Fax: 020 8742 8390
Email: *mail@lettsed.co.uk*
Website: *www.letts-education.com*

First published 2001
Reprinted 2002

Text © Steve Foster and Judith Polley 2001

British Library Cataloging in Publication Data. A CIP record of this book is available from the British Library.

ISBN 1 84085 635 1

Letts Educational Limited is a division of Granada Learning Limited, part of the Granada Media Group.

Edited and typeset by Cambridge Publishing Management
Designed by Moondisks Limited

English
Book 1 Ages 13–14

Introduction 5

Each unit in this book is targeted at one of the following areas of the Key Stage 3 Literacy Framework: Word level (W), Sentence level (S), Text level – Reading (TR) or Text level – Writing (TW)

Unit 1   Parts of speech (W) 6

Unit 2   Spelling strategies (W) 10

Unit 3   Common errors (W) 12

Unit 4   The apostrophe (W) 14

Unit 5   The roots of English (W) 16

SURVIVAL SHEET 1

Parts of speech 18

Unit 6   Standard English (W) 20

Unit 7   Punctuation (S) 22

Unit 8   Paragraphing (S) 24

Unit 9   Figures of speech (S) 26

Unit 10   Sentence construction (S) 28

Unit 11   Use of quotations (S) 30

SURVIVAL SHEET 2

Standard English .32

Unit 12   Strategies for effective reading (S) 34

Unit 13   Studying persuasive texts (S) . . .36

Unit 14   Reading non-fiction (S) 38

Unit 15   Studying poetry (S) 40

Unit 16   The front page (TR) 42

Unit 17   Presentation in other forms (TR) .44

Unit 18   Reading Shakespeare (TR) 46

Unit 19   Reading in paper 1 (1) (TW) 48

Unit 20   Reading in paper 1 (2) (TW) 50

SURVIVAL SHEET 3

Reading checklist .52

Unit 21   Strategies for writing (TW) 54

Unit 22   Writing poetry (TW) 56

Unit 23   Writing a script (TW) 58

Unit 24   Imaginative and narrative writing (TW) 60

Unit 25   Descriptive writing (TW) 62

Unit 26   Persuasive and argumentative writing (TW) 64

Unit 27   Presentation of ideas (TW) 66

Unit 28   Letters and diaries (TW) 68

SURVIVAL SHEET 4

Writing checklist .70

SURVIVAL SHEET 5

Getting top marks 72

Unit 29   Hotseating (TW) 74

Unit 30   Presenting a poem (TW) 76

Unit 31   Formal activities (TW) 78

Unit 32   Giving a talk (TW) 80

Test paper 1 82

Test paper 2 86

Answers 90

Notes 93

Jargon Buster 94

Index 96

Introduction

This book has been written especially for you. It has been designed to help you in your English lessons throughout Year 9 and it contains material that will provide you with support as you follow the National Literacy Strategy and prepare for the National Tests in May.

It is not meant to be used as a textbook. Although there are questions, tests and practice sections, these are only included in case you feel you need them.

You could read this book right through from cover to cover. Don't! Instead, skim through it to see what it contains and the way it is organised. Try to become familiar with the Contents list. Find sections that would be helpful to you at this stage in your course, or areas where you know you need help. Begin by studying those.

As the course goes on, you will find other sections that will help you. For any task you are set, there is advice and support in each of the main units. Look carefully at the Word, Sentence and Text levels before attempting any piece of work.

There are also special features on certain subjects and advice on preparing for the National Tests. It is very important to remember that no book can replace the help and advice of your teacher, nor will you be able to use this book effectively if you do not have a good knowledge of your chosen Shakespeare text.

The main aim of this book is to help and encourage you in your study of the English language. It is a fascinating and, sometimes, frustrating subject. It has strict rules – which are broken regularly! Hopefully, you will develop both an interest and ability in the language that will continue to improve beyond Year 9 and stay with you into your adult life.

Parts of speech

A *noun* is a person, a place, or a thing;
Feelings, ideas, a cat or a king.
John, himself, is him or he,
Pronouns replace nouns, you see.
A big fat *adjective* (or maybe five)   5
Comes with a *noun* or *pronoun* to
    describe.
Is, was, has, jump, play, observe,
Every sentence needs a *verb*.

Adverbs tell you when, where, how,
Quickly, upstairs, soon and now.   10
In, on, under, up, and down,
Prepositions when before a *noun*.
And, or, but, are called *conjunctions*,
To connect and link are their main
    functions.
To yell out, with no other connections,   15
'Ouch!' and 'Darn it!' are *interjections*.

Anonymous

This short, fun poem about the parts of speech offers one way of learning the names of the different parts of speech and their function in sentences. The full list and their definitions are given over the next few pages. (Their initials spell the word 'CANVIPPA' which might help you to remember them all.)

C Connective or
**   conjunction**
A connective or
conjunction is a word
that joins or links
sentences together.

Example

She ran home *and* made her sister's sandwiches.
I am always happy *when* she is here.
When she is here, I am always happy.

Exercise 1

Read the following paragraph and suggest the part of speech of each of the ten underlined words.

The <u>camel</u> was one of the most <u>interesting</u> <u>animals</u> that we saw <u>in</u> the zoo. <u>Unfortunately</u>, <u>it</u> <u>was</u> <u>soon</u> time to go home, and we hadn't had time to see everything. <u>Perhaps</u> we will see more <u>next</u> time.

I   camel – noun

A Adverb

Adverbs usually tell us more about the action of the verb.

> ### Example
>
> He ran *quickly*.
> They talked *noisily*.
> The tortoise moved *awkwardly*.

N Noun

A noun is a word that names a person or object or emotion.

> ### Example
>
> The *girl* loved her *father*.
> *Henry* saw the *light*.
> *Love* is all that counts.

V Verb

A verb is a word that indicates the action or 'state of being' in a sentence.

> ### Example
>
> She *came* home.
> He *is* sad.
> It *was* getting late.

Exercise 2

Identify the part of speech of each underlined word.

1 Monaya loved the <u>toy</u>. (noun)
2 <u>Kate</u> rarely left home without the teddy.
3 The plane flew over the <u>range</u> of mountains.
4 Where did <u>she</u> go?
5 <u>Sometimes</u> he talked too loudly.
6 Peter struggled to <u>work</u> out the sums.
7 She went home <u>and</u> had her tea.
8 The dentist examined the <u>false</u> teeth.
9 She stood <u>before</u> the window.
10 Abdur batted <u>carelessly</u>.

RED   The 'work' that a word does in a sentence determines   **RED**
its part of speech.

I Interjection

An interjection is a word that is usually an exclamation.

> ### Example
>
> Good heavens!   Well done!   Wow!
> Oh no!   Urgh!   Goodness!

P Pronoun

A pronoun is a word that is used in place of a noun.

> ### Example
>
> Harold loved *her*.
> Happily, *she* loved *him* back!

P Preposition

A word functions as a preposition when it comes in front of a noun or a pronoun in a phrase.

> ### Example
>
> The man walked *down* the road.
> The submarine dived *under* the sea.
> *Between* you and me, I think we should be told.

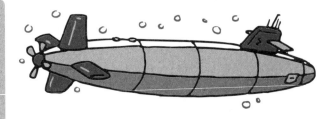

Exercise 3

Use each of the following nouns in different ways, by giving them different functions within a sentence. Then identify how you have used them. The first is done for you.

1   book – He opened the *book*. (noun)
     Can you *book* me a flight? (verb)
     He was a *book* fanatic. (adjective)

2   tie

3   film

4   flower

5   picture

6   face

A Adjective

An adjective is a word that describes a noun.

The same word might be a different part of speech depending on how it is used in different sentences.

> ### Example
> It was a *beautiful* sunset.
> The cake was *delicious*.
> I feel *happy*.

> ### Example
> 1 He sat on the *chair*.
> 2 Shall I *chair* the meeting for you?
> 3 The *chair* leg broke.

In each case the function (grammatical part of speech) of the word *chair* is different.

1 The word *chair* functions as a name. (noun)
2 The word *chair* functions as an action. (verb)
3 The word *chair* functions as a descriptive word. (adjective)

So, a noun in English could function as a verb or an adjective as well.

Subject and objects
Consider this sentence:

> ### Example
> John loved his sister.

John is the subject of the verb *loved*, and the person he loves, his *sister*, is the object.

Exercise 4

Pronouns change according to whether they are the subject or object in a sentence.
Notice how *I* becomes *me* in these two sentences:
I love Rosie.
Rosie loves me.

Fill in the missing pronouns.

1 George loves Edwina and Edwina loves <u>him</u> back!

2 They saw the shark and it saw _____ !

3 You would like the Smiths. _____ are lovely people.

4 He noticed Philippa and watched _____ carefully.

5 As the taxi approached, he waved _____ down.

Spelling strategies and rules

The rules of English spelling are complicated as it is a complicated language, developed down the centuries from a wide variety of influences. Rules exist for us to check whether we have got things right. But there are exceptions to every rule – and these must be learned too!

The trouble with English spelling is that much of it dates from before the alterations in the language in the fifteenth century, so that today's spelling often reflects the way words were pronounced in Chaucer's time.

When faced with a new word, we tend to try to spell the word as it is pronounced. This is not a great idea since one in five words is not spelled as it sounds and many of the words we use most commonly are irregular. This leads to the misleading impression that English spelling is a completely random ordering of letters – which it is not!

We can do something to improve our ability to spell accurately but the approach we must use is a mixed one. We need to understand the principles that underlie spelling so that we can apply them to our writing. Whenever we misspell a word there is always a reason. We need to know *why* we spelt that word wrongly in *that* way, then we can begin to tackle our real problems. Spelling is a matter of pride. If you take pride in your work, you will want it to be spelt as accurately as possible. You do not want errors to detract from what you are communicating. There are a variety of techniques to help you improve your spelling.

Exercise 1

The statements below are based on the three paragraphs above. Write *true* or *false* after each one.

1   We do not need to learn the exceptions to rules. (false)

2   Today's spellings were affected by changes in Chaucer's time.

3   There is no sense in English spelling.

4   There is always a reason for a spelling mistake.

5   Pride in your work produces good spelling.

RED ALERT *Separate* has a *rat* in it. *Necessary* is like an old-fashioned **AL** shirt – it has one collar and two *studs*!

Spelling strategies

- Have a dictionary or Spell-well at your side.
- Try to learn as many spelling rules as possible.
- Ask a parent or friend to check your work.
- Do word-games: crosswords are very helpful since you cannot arrive at a completed answer if the spelling is incorrect.
- Play dictionary games: ask a friend to open a page at random and try to spell the first ten entries.
- Whenever you ask for help in spelling a word, always write down the way you think it should be spelt and then compare your version with the one you are given – you will never spell well if you rely on others supplying the right answer all the time.
- With new words:

Look at the word. **Cover** the word. **Write** the word. **Check** what you've written.

The key spelling rules

- Write *i* before *e* except after *c*, when the sound is 'ee':
  believe thief chief grief ceiling conceive receive receipt
  Exceptions: seize sheikh weird weir
- Words ending in *l* and adding *-ly* become *-lly*:
  faithful – faithfully   beautiful – beautifully
- Words ending with a consonant followed by *y* drop the *y* and add *-ies*:
  quarry – quarries   ferry – ferries   lavatory – lavatories
- Words ending with a vowel followed by *y*, add an *s*:
  valley – valleys   day – days   trolley – trolleys

Exercise 2

Correct the spelling errors in this list.

1 recived (received)
2 beatiful
3 sincerly
4 trollys
5 chieves
6 wierd
7 neice
8 totaly
9 traveler
10 cheries

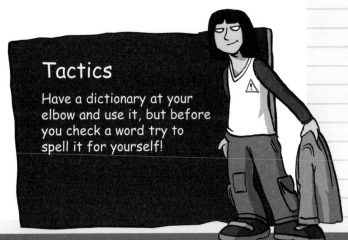

Tactics

Have a dictionary at your elbow and use it, but before you check a word try to spell it for yourself!

Common errors

You need to be aware of the following words which frequently catch out even the most careful of writers.

A	accept – except	access – excess	advice – advise	affect – effect
	alley – ally	aloud – allowed	altar – alter	angle – angel
B	bass – base	bare – bear	boarder – border	boy – buoy
	break – brake	breath – breathe	buy – by	
C	cease – seize	cemetery – symmetry	cereal – serial	cite – sight – site
	clothes – cloths	course – coarse	complement – compliment	
	cue – queue	currant – current		
D	deceased – diseased	decent – descent – dissent		
	desert – dessert	drawers – draws		
E	eligible – illegible	emigrant – immigrant		
	envelop – envelope			
F	fare – fair	farther – father		
	fiancé – fiancée	formally – formerly		
	forth – fourth			
G	gilt – guilt	gorilla – guerrilla		
H	hear – here	him – hymn		
	hoard – horde	human – humane		
	hole – whole			

Exercise 1

Fill in the correct word missing in each of these sentences. Look up the words in the dictionary if you are unsure which is the right choice. The first letter has been given.

1 They were all there, except my brother.
2 Anna bought a new chest of d_____.
3 Alexis could go no f_____.
4 "I_____ a boy," said the midwife.
5 Siobhan walked p_____ the shop.
6 A large p_____ of birthday cake awaited her.
7 The cemetery was a very q_____ place.
8 June opened the s_____ cupboard and took out a new packet of envelopes.
9 The Kahns' friends admired t_____ new house.
10 There w_____ too many apples to carry in one hand.

I	imminent – eminent	implicit – explicit	ingenious – ingenuous	its – it's
L	later – latter	lightening – lightning	loose – lose	
	luxuriant – luxurious			
M	magnate – magnet	medal – meddle	miner – minor	moral – morale
N	new – knew			
P	passed – past	peace – piece	peal – peel	
	personal – personnel	practice – practise	principal – principle	
Q	quiet – quite			
R	rain – reign – rein	recent – resent		
S	sew – sow	stationary – stationery		
	steal – steel	suit – suite		
T	their – there – they're			
	to – too – two			
W	waist – waste			
	ware – wear – were – where			
	weather – whether	witch – which		
	who's – whose			
Y	your – you're			

Exercise 2

Using the list of common errors, fill in the missing word.

1 For <u>dessert</u> they had lemon meringue pie.

2 The illegal _____ was arrested at Dover.

3 My guardian _____ watches over me constantly.

4 Sidra slipped on his_____ from the mountain top.

5 The _____ on Doris's old skirt was too small.

6 A sudden flash of _____ illuminated the countryside.

7 Bad _____ invariably interrupts Test cricket!

8 She stood there, as _____ as a mouse.

9 Che Guevara was a professional _____.

10 The snooker player carefully chalked his _____.

13

The apostrophe

The apostrophe in English is used in two main ways:

1 To show where a letter or letters have been left out
   This is most commonly seen in speech where we shorten words.

> ### Example
>
> I'm (I am)   can't (cannot)
> they're (they are)   I won't (I will not)

It is acceptable to use shortened forms like these when you are writing down what has actually been spoken. You should not, however, use them other than for speech.

The apostrophe is also used in the shortening of some 'poetic' words:

> ### Example
>
> ne'er (never)   e'er (ever)

Exercise 1

Place the apostrophe in the correct place in the *italicised* word.

 1 Mother took her *sons* hand.
    Mother took her son's hand.
 2 *You're* just who I was looking for!
 3 Neeta loved *Peters* haircut.
 4 The wind blew off the *girls* hats.
 5 It was a *days* work to get it done.
 6 *Jesus* disciples were mainly fishermen.
 7 The *fishs* head lay on the plate.
 8 The *sheeps* wool was laid on the bench.
 9 We all went to *Spurs* match against United.
10 She spilt paint on her *teachers* shoes.

14

Only use apostrophes if you are sure where they go. You are more likely to be right than wrong if you *never* use them!

2 To indicate possession or ownership

This is the most difficult of all the uses of the apostrophe to master.
Here are some examples of the correct use.

Example

a) In the singular: 's
   The boy's book. (the book of the boy)
   The cat's bowl. (the bowl of the cat)

Example

b) In the plural: ' after the s
   The teachers' room. (the room of the
   teachers)
   The girls' scooters. (the scooters of
   the girls)

Example

c) Where a noun does not take a plural
   ending in s, 's is used in the singular
   and plural
   The man's suit. (the suit of the man)
   The men's suits. (the suits of the men)

Example

d) Where a word already ends in s,
   add 's
   James's house
   the Jones's dog

Sometimes an apostrophe is added without
an extra s, e.g. James'. This is acceptable,
but adding an apostrophe + s is seen as
correct.

Exercise 2

Copy out this passage, inserting the apostrophes in the correct places.

Of all my mother's friends, I liked Emily most
of all. She lived in a row of fishermen's
cottages in Bideford and loved to
talk about the hard times of her
youth. "Have you ever had water
soup?" she asked me one day.
 "What you do is boil a pan of
water then sprinkle it with salt and
pepper. You eat it with bread. Delicious.
What you can't eat, you put in the cat's bowl."

15

The roots of English

Understanding the jargon

A prefix is a syllable or syllables with a set meaning that are added to the beginning of a word:
  anti- (meaning against) as in *anticlockwise*; *hyper-* (meaning over or excessive) as in *hyperactive*.
A suffix is a syllable or syllables with a set meaning which are added to the end of a word:
  -ness (*kind + ness = kindness*).
A plural is more than one: *dog/dogs, baby/babies*.
Vowels are the letters *a, e, i, o* and *u*.
Consonants are all of letters of the alphabet apart from the vowels.
A syllable is each unit of sound in a word as you say it is a syllable: *but/ter* has two syllables.

English is one of the most popular languages in the world. The reason for this is that it is always altering to meet the changing demands of daily life. Over the years, some words die out and others are born. The ingredients that make up the word television have existed since ancient times – *tele* is from a Greek word meaning 'from afar', and *vision* is taken from the Latin verb *video* which means 'I see'. And so a new word was created from these smaller parts to describe a machine that neither the Greeks nor the Romans could ever have imagined.

Other words change their meaning but stay in use. The word *gay* originally meant 'bright' or 'cheerful', whereas nowadays it describes someone who prefers a same-sex relationship. A word like *decimate* has changed its meaning almost by mistake. Literally, it means 'to reduce by one-tenth' though people generally use it to mean 'to reduce *to* one-tenth'.

Exercise 1

Based on the information on this page and the next, and using a bit of deduction, and *without* the use of a dictionary, write down what you think the following words mean.

1 hydrant – pipe from a water main
2 thermometer
3 dehydration
4 viaduct
5 speedometer

Derivations of words

Many of our words come from Greek and Latin. By knowing their origins it is often easier to understand how they come to be spelt as they are in modern English. The list below provides common root words with an example of their usage today.

agr/o (field, farming)	agriculture	dys (bad)	dyslexia
ambi (both)	ambidextrous	frater/fratr (brother)	fratricide
ante (before)	antenatal	gyn/o/ae (woman)	misogyny, gynaecologist
anti (against)	antidote	haemo (blood)	haemophilia
arch/ae/o (old)	archaeology	hydr/o (water)	hydraulic
astro (star)	astrology	hypo (under)	hypodermic
audio (hear)	audiotape	logy (study of)	geology
bi (two)	bicycle	mater/matr (mother)	maternal
bio (life)	biology	mega (many)	megalith
		milli (one thousandth)	millimetre
		neo (new)	neolithic

cardi/o (heart)	cardiogram		
centi (one hundred)	century		
chrono (time)	chronology	omni (all)	omnibus
cide (killing)	infanticide	pater, patr (father)	paternal
crypto (hidden)	cryptic	phil (love)	bibliophile
deca (ten)	decagon	poly (many)	polyglot
dexter/dextr (right)	dextral	quad (four)	quadrangle
dox (opinion)	orthodox	retro (backwards)	retrospect
duct (lead)	aqueduct	tele (from afar)	television

Exercise 2

Who or what are killed in these 'cide' crimes?

1 matricide (mother)
2 suicide
3 parricide
4 regicide
5 fratricide
6 genocide
7 spermicide
8 herbicide
9 homicide
10 insecticide

Parts of speech

Now that you have covered a wide variety of topics, here is a summary of the essential survival points.

Parts of speech

- There are eight parts of speech and they are used to describe the work a word does within a sentence. (Remember 'CANVIPPA'.)
- Don't worry if you can't remember all of them since you will not be tested on them in your National Tests.
- It is useful to know the names of parts of speech since you can use the technical terms to identify the functions of words.
- It is vital to learn parts of speech when you learn a foreign language, as by understanding the grammar of your own language you can begin to understand the different rules that apply in another.
- Foreign languages are *not* straight word-for-word translations.

Spelling strategies

- Many words are spelled as they are pronounced but twenty percent of all words are not spelled as they sound.
- Good spelling is vital when presenting our work as it reflects well on ourselves. Many people take a dim view of poor spelling and this reflects badly on you and your work.
- Take pride in your work: make sure it is as good as possible at all times – and that means spelling accurately.
- Learn and make use of spelling strategies to help improve your spelling.

Common errors

- Words that sound the same but are spelled differently are known as homophones, for example *new/knew, bare/bear*. Take care and use the correct spelling.

The apostrophe

- This is a difficult punctuation mark to master. If you do not know where to use the apostrophe – leave it out!

The roots of English

- Study the lists of important root words from which modern English draws its sources to help you spell and decipher new words.
- When you discover and understand a new word, try to find an opportunity to use it.

Standard English

A brief history of the English language

English has been spoken for over fourteen centuries though there have been so many changes in sounds, vocabulary and grammar that its earliest form is effectively a foreign language. The first significant invasions of Britain occurred during the sixth and seventh centuries with the arrival of the Angles, Saxons and Jutes. They came from different dialect areas in Germany: the East Saxons, South Saxons and West Saxons who live on in Essex, Sussex and Wessex. Predictably enough, the East Angles were located in East Anglia, whilst the Middle Angles settled in Mercia and Northumbria.

The institution of the Church in England, following the arrival of St Augustine from Rome in 599 AD, was an important feature of our early language development. The monks were the first writers to use the Roman alphabet. The Scandinavian raids from the eighth century and the subsequent settlement of the Danelaw – a line running from Chester to London – created the original North-South divide.

The Norman Conquest in 1066 brought a major new influence, French, which became the language of the law and the court. The Norman scribes put the native English they heard on paper, and this is when the first oddities in spelling occur.

In 1476 William Caxton introduced the printing press which led to standardisation in spelling. The two key influences in the sixteenth and seventeenth centuries were William Shakespeare (1564–1616) and the King

Exercise 1

Write *true* or *false* after each of these statements.

1   We wouldn't understand the English of King Alfred. (true)

2   Essex girls were originally East Saxons.

3   Latin was written in the monasteries.

4   The Danelaw marks the North from the South.

5   The Normans spoke French.

James Bible, or Authorised Version (1611). Shakespeare put so many words and expressions into print for the first time that he has had a lasting effect upon our daily lives. The Authorised Version gave us a variety of sayings such as 'an eye for an eye' and 'blind leading the blind'.

In the last two centuries English has become a world language. The British Empire retreated in the middle of the twentieth century but it left English wherever it had been. It is estimated that a third of the world's population, over two billion people, use English regularly in their daily lives, and with the fastest-growing form of communication – the internet – having English as its basic language, English is certain to be ever more popular in the future.

Dialect and accent

A dialect is the type of English that is spoken in your locality. A Devonian uses different words and arranges them in a different way from someone who grows up in Yorkshire, for example. Most counties have their own dialect preservation societies which try to keep their dialects alive. In this day and age, the influence of the television, radio and pop music means that we are exposed to a far greater range of vocabulary and expressions than was common before the mid-twentieth century. This is neither a good nor a bad thing – it is the way things are. Our language is a living one which survives as all living things survive, by changing to meet changing circumstances.

There was a time when a southern accent was considered superior to those of other parts of the country. Happily, things have changed and nowadays all accents are equally valuable.

Exercise 2

Write *true* or *false* after each of these statements.

1   Shakespeare created the first English dictionary. (false)

2   The Bible gave us 'an eye for an eye'.

3   Doctor Johnson was a lexicographer.

4   Pop music kills dialects.

5   We all need posh accents.

Punctuation

Punctuation is the most difficult aspect of writing. Written English and spoken English are different languages. When you speak, the object is to convey an idea from your brain to that of your listener. In order to do so, you have a whole range of things other than words to help you: the tone of your voice, the look on your face and the way you use your body to name but three.

When you write, you have merely the words. Into them must go all the expression that body language gives to your speech.

Read this sentence:

> **Example**
>
> I like fish and chips and cake.

As it is written, the sentence suggests that the speaker enjoys a very strange pile of food on her plate. Once you put in the punctuation marks, however, the sense becomes clear.

Now we know that the speaker is describing two sorts of food that he or she likes.
Once we grasp that punctuation is used to help the reader make sense of what is written, we are well on the way to improving our handling of the different punctuation marks.

> **Example**
>
> I like fish and chips, and cake.

Exercise 1

Read the following passage and insert the correct punctuation. If you know how, start new paragraphs in the right places, too.

can I have a wasp please asked the little lad but we don't sell them said the pet shop owner we sell budgies canaries mice and snakes but no wasps that's funny said the little lad you've got one in the window

> "Can I have a wasp, please?" ...

RED ALERT When you are writing out conversations, always start a new paragraph for each new speech. This rule makes it quite plain who is speaking. **AL**

The full stop (.), question mark (?) and exclamation mark (!)

Each of these marks has a full stop included in its make-up so each of them is used to signal the end of a sentence.

The comma (,)

The comma is used to make meaning clear by separating words and phrases that might be confused.

The colon (:) and the semi colon (;)

The colon introduces a list or an example whilst the semi colon separates lists of phrases or short sentences just as a comma separates lists of words.

Inverted commas, speech marks, quotation marks (' ' or " ")

These three terms all mean the same thing – they indicate the words actually spoken by a person in a conversation.

The dash (–)

It introduces something that is unexpected.

The apostrophe (')

Apostrophes are used to indicate contractions or possession (see pages 14–15).

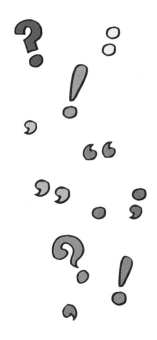

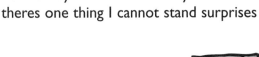

Punctuate the following advice.

The dash introduces something unexpected beware of overuse since it can easily replace all sorts of other punctuation marks and gives the writing a sloppy feel here is an example of how it may be used effectively
theres one thing I cannot stand surprises

Paragraphing

The paragraph as a visual aid

Open any book and look at the way in which the page is broken up by the use of paragraphs. One use of paragraphs is to provide visual interest for the reader. If the printed page is one solid chunk of writing, you are immediately daunted by the prospect of having to read it.

Paragraphs also help to break up information into sections. In an argumentative essay, they will indicate the stages of the arguments for and against. In a piece of personal writing, they will reflect different stages of thought or description as the writing unfolds.

The National Curriculum expects you to demonstrate:

- The ability to shape ideas into paragraphs which relate to the specific task;

- The ability to show different ways of opening and linking paragraphs;

- The ability to understand how a writer connects paragraphs by using linking words.

Exercise 1

Read these paragraphs. Underline any linking words or phrases.

The issue of euthanasia has been much in the news lately. As medicine keeps patients alive longer, people are becoming worried that their suffering might be prolonged.

On the other hand, unscrupulous people may use euthanasia as a way to persuade older people that they should take the easy way out of life.

The unscrupulous people might, however, be using the kind nature of the older person to hasten their ending – and thus rid themselves of the trouble of caring for the patient.

Paragraphs in the planning stage

When you are producing a piece of descriptive or personal writing, it is vital that you prepare a plan before you start the task.

Imagine you are given the essay title: 'A day at the beach'. One very obvious way is to look at the beach at different times of the day: you could start in the early morning and end late at night, waiting for the cycle to begin all over again. The paragraphs would be easy to organise; they would divide neatly into four or five periods of the day.

Another way to do it might be to start at the end of the day and take the description right back to the beginning:

Example

Night falls. The beach fades into darkness.

The length of a paragraph

There is no set length for a paragraph. It may be six pages long (if you do not mind boring your reader to death!) or it may just be a single word. A single-word paragraph, by the way, is a very dramatic opening to a story. Think of the possibilities of a story starting *Fire!* The safest advice is to remember to use paragraphs, and aim to make a variety of lengths since this will give your writing an interesting rhythm – sometimes slow, at other times lively and fast-moving as appropriate.

Exercise 2

Put these paragraphs in a sensible order.

A I look forward to welcoming you as a BBC Diamond Credit Cardholder.

B Naturally, I am disappointed at the closure of the credit card. However, we would like you to know how much we appreciate your valuable custom so we would like to extend to you the opportunity to join the Bloodsuckers Banking Company's credit card scheme.

C You may be aware that the Travellers' Hotel group is being sold and that the Travellers' credit card will cease to exist after 13 July. You will be able to use it until 30 June.

D The BBC's card offers you a wide range of benefits including the chance to earn valuable Bus Miles which you can use on local buses anywhere in the Soho area. Simply complete the pre-paid application form enclosed and your account will be credited immediately with 50 Bus Miles.

Figures of speech

Understanding the jargon

A metaphor is a figure of speech in which a word or phrase is likened to something it does not literally denote.

A simile is like a metaphor but uses the phrase *as ... as a ...*

Literal expression

The boy ran along the road is literal. In other words, each word means exactly what it says. It is plain and to the point. Such writing is needed when you are asked to convey facts but it is very boring to read. For that reason, writers employ a whole range of techniques to make their writing more interesting and imaginative.

Figurative language

Figurative language involves the reader's imagination. Since you are more likely to respond positively to something that has made you think, writers use figures of speech almost automatically. This involvement of the reader in creating the book is reminiscent of the little boy who said that he thought radio plays were better than film or television 'because they have the best scenery'.

You will come across many figures of speech in literature. At this stage, you need only concern yourself with a few of them.

Exercise 1

Identify the similes or metaphors in the following sentences. The first is done for you.

1   The sun smiled upon us that day.

'The sun smiled' is not a comparison between one word and another. We know that the sun is not *actually* smiling, but it has been given that characteristic. It is a metaphor.

2   The athlete ran like the wind.
3   The boxer fought like a tiger.
4   The daffodils danced in the breeze.
5   The freezing wind cut into their protective clothes.
6   The roads were choked with traffic.

- Simile and metaphor – two commonly used figures of speech that compare one thing to another. For example: Julie sings *like an angel.*

Like an angel suggests a comparison between two things, in this case a Julie and an angel. This comparison is known as a simile. A simile is usually introduced by *like* or *as*.

You could take this a stage further. For example: Julie is *an angel.*

Here Julie is said to be something she cannot possibly be – an angel. This comparison, where we say one thing is another, is called a metaphor. So we could call a metaphor a condensed simile.

- Alliteration – the repetition of similar sounds for effect. For example: The *sh*iny *s*erpent *sl*ithered *sl*owly.

- Onomatopoeia – the use of words that closely imitate the sounds made. For example: The cat *hissed* and *spat* at its attacker.

- Personification – the use of an abstract feeling or emotion as if it is a living or animate thing. For example: *Laughter* shone in their eyes.

- Hyperbole – an obvious over-exaggeration. For example: *Thousands* of wasps descended on our picnic.

Exercise 2

Identify the personification and hyperbole in these sentences.

1   The sun smiled upon the happy couple. (personification)

2   There were millions of cockroaches in the apartment.

3   Famine crept through the enemy camp.

4   The icy fingers of dawn frosted the bedroom windows.

5   Mum, you never say a nice thing about me.

Sentence construction

Types of sentence

There are four types of sentence:

The statement

> **Example**
>
> He made a steam engine.

The command

> **Example**
>
> Leave that alone.

The question

> **Example**
>
> Where are you going?

The exclamation

> **Example**
>
> Well, I'll be darned!

Simple sentences

Simple sentences can be made more interesting if they are joined together, often by connectives and/or pronouns. Read the passage opposite.

> **Example**
>
> Seema came into the room. Seema had forgotten what she wanted. Seema walked out into the garden. She enjoyed a stroll in the sunshine.

Exercise 1

Add connectives to make the following pieces of writing more interesting.

1 The dog was getting wet in the rain. The dog howled to be let in. There was no one in to hear the dog.

> The dog was getting wet in the rain and soon he howled to be let in, but there was no one in to hear him.

2 Beethoven is considered to be a great composer. Beethoven wrote a wide range of music. Sadly, Beethoven became deaf.

3 The gardener was mowing the lawn. It started to rain. The gardener put away her tools.

The repetition of the noun *Seema* is tiresome as are the short sentences. You could make the writing more interesting:

> ## Example
>
> Seema came into the room. However, she had forgotten what she wanted, so she walked out into the garden where she enjoyed a stroll in the sunshine.

Complex sentences

A complex sentence is one in which there is a single main clause and one or more subordinate clauses. In this example the main clause is italicised.

> ## Example
>
> *I cannot bear it* when it rains and when I have nothing to do.

A different effect is achieved when the main clause is placed at the end. This is known as a periodic statement and has a more weighty feel to it. It is the sentence structure which was used in classical literature:

When you shape your sentences, it would clearly become rather tedious always to follow the same pattern. Now you understand the difference between types of sentence, the advice is to use a variety!

> ## Example
>
> When it rains and I have nothing to do, I cannot bear it.

Exercise 2

Fill in the missing words.

Always try to get some (_____) in your sentence construction. The first sentences that children use often consist of (_____) ideas which are joined together by the (_____) 'and'. The little child might write: 'I got up and I had my breakfast and I went to school.' By the time (_____) adults reach the sophisticated heights of Year 9, their (_____) is far less simple: 'When yours (_____) had exhausted the possibilities of (_____) repose, I roused myself, presented myself at the family (_____) for a modest repast of scrambled (_____) on toast. That finished, I assumed my outdoor garb and set off to receive the applause and (_____) of my teachers.'

RED   **Variety is the spice of life – and it certainly makes sentences more enjoyable!**   RED

Use of quotations

When you are writing about a book, play or poem you have read, the quotation is your strongest weapon. The teacher or examiner wishes to know your opinion about a character, a story line or theme; by using quotations you show that you can handle the material you have read in such a way as to make a point.

Keep quotations short

By and large, the shorter a quotation, the more effective it is. When you are writing about your Shakespeare play in the National Test, you will be able to use the actual extract from the scene in the examination. Common sense tells you that there is little point in writing out twenty lines and saying, 'You learn a lot about Macbeth's character from these lines'. For a start, it wastes valuable time spending it carefully copying out all that poetry. More importantly, there is no point in telling the examiner that he or she can learn a lot from those lines. The examiner is interested in what you, the student, have learned!

Quotations for *Romeo and Juliet*

Let us look at one of the questions on *Romeo and Juliet* that was set in a recent National Test. In the scene studied, Juliet has just bidden a long, tearful farewell to Romeo at the end of their wedding night. Her parents find her weeping and assume it is because of the death of her cousin, Tybalt, killed by Romeo. In order to cheer her up (!), they tell her that they have brought forward her wedding to Paris. They are surprised that she is so angry with them and the scene ends with the Nurse, who knows all about Romeo, advising Juliet to marry Paris. Juliet's friendship with the Nurse is abruptly terminated.

Exercise 1

Read the following speech and summarise it in as few words as possible.

O Romeo, Romeo! Wherefore art thou Romeo?

Deny thy father, and refuse thy name;

Or, if thou wilt not, be but sworn my love,

And I'll no longer be a Capulet.

Use a highlighter pen when studying text to mark up the important lines, phrases and words. AL

The task set on this scene is; 'How does Shakespeare make you feel increasingly sympathetic towards Juliet in this scene?' Consider the wording: 'increasingly sympathetic'. Naturally you would feel sympathetic towards her but how does Shakespeare stoke up the sympathy?

The best way to tackle this is to go through the scene with a highlighter pen. Use the pen to highlight quickly what you feel is important. Then list the words and phrases that might make Juliet feel unhappy and so make us feel sorry for her:

- Her mother calls Romeo a *villain* and Juliet is deeply in love with him!
- Her mother promises to have Romeo killed: *he will keep Tybalt company.*
- Her mother says Paris will soon *make thee ... a joyful bride.*
- Her father enters fuming that *Juliet doth ... not give us thanks.*
- He leaves promising to let her *die in the streets* if she rejects Paris.
- The Nurse completes her misery by declaring of Paris: *O, he's a lovely gentleman!/Romeo's a dishclout to him.*

The golden rules of quotation
- Keep them as short as possible: incorporating a single word into your sentence shows that your words and Shakespeare's are completely in harmony: *Romeo is a 'villain'*
- Quote exactly what is written in the original.
- If you wish to use a quote and a word or expression does not fit in comfortably, leave it out and put three dots to show the omission.
- You should always lay out poetry exactly as it appears in the original. If Shakespeare wrote two lines of poetry and you quote them, you can either write them out on two separate lines or you can run both lines together but put a slash mark where one line ends and the next begins.

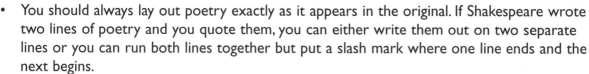

Exercise 2

Put // at the end of each line of verse in the following quotation from *Romeo and Juliet*, Act II Scene I, then check your text to see if you have got it right.

It is too rash, too unadvis'd, too sudden; too like the lightning, which doth cease to be ere one can say 'It lightens'. Sweet, good-night! This bud of love, by summer's ripening breath, May prove a beauteous flower when next we meet.

Now do the same with this passage from *Twelfth Night*, Act I Scene I.

O, when mine eyes did see Olivia first, Methought she purg'd the air of pestilence! That instant was I turn'd into a hart; and my desires, like fell and cruel hounds, e'er since pursue me.

Standard English

- English is a rich language, which has evolved over the years with all sorts of influences from all over the world. We owe a great debt to writers such as Shakespeare and Doctor Johnson, the former for giving us so many everyday words and expressions, the latter for being the first man to create a dictionary of our language.

- English is the only true international language. We do not own English and must be prepared for other nations to change it as they see fit – and we can adopt their uses if we feel it makes our language stronger!

- All of us have different dialects, that is, variations in expression. The way we pronounce our words is our accent and this helps to give interest and life to speech.

- Read the best writers to see the most effective written English at work. We all learn by copying others and reading the best will help us to write the best!

Punctuation

- Accurate punctuation is a difficult skill that is worth accomplishing. When we write, we are trying to convey an idea or ideas to our readers. Punctuation is the tool we use to make sense of what we write. If we are hopeless with punctuation, then people will not be able to understand what we are writing.

- Do not just sprinkle punctuation marks anywhere like pepper and salt. Put them where you feel they will do some work!

Paragraphing

- A piece of writing without paragraphs is very hard on the eye since no one likes to read solid blocks of print.

- Paragraphs should enable the reader to see the organisation of the writing, with a clear passage set aside for an opening, and similarly a clear ending signalled in the same way. Each paragraph should centre on a particular aspect of the writing.

Figures of speech

- Figurative language gives life and interest to your writing. Most figures of speech involve the reader making a comparison between something happening in a story and something else that we all know.

- Make your reader think about what you are writing by challenging him or her with different and fresh comparisons.

Sentence constructions

- The inexperienced writer tends to write in simple, short sentences. This is effective. The meaning is clear. You can read it quickly. Such writing can be boring!

- Learn and practise the techniques for running together a number of ideas in a single sentence.

- The important thing is that your writing flows smoothly. You need to learn the wide range of ways in which clauses can be joined to form exactly the right relationship between one idea and another.

Use of quotations

- The brief quotation is the perfect tool for the student. A well-chosen quotation tells the examiner that the student has understood exactly what is required and that they can use not just their own words but those of the writer to make their point!

Strategies for effective reading

After nine years at school you have acquired some advanced reading skills. As time goes on these will develop further as you experience new forms of writing. The wider the range of writing you meet, the easier English will become.

In the same way that you probably use different styles of handwriting for different tasks, so you need to adopt various approaches to reading. You will have been expected to skim and scan texts for basic meaning. You will have been set exercises in putting paragraphs and sections in order, or sequencing. You will know how to look at a passage with some of the words missing and work out what the missing word might be. This is known as a cloze exercise and requires that you study words in context, or where they are placed. You will be aware of what is meant by fiction and non-fiction and have been asked to complete some close reading.

In Year 9 you will be expected to read and analyse texts, both in class and on your own, with a high level of competence. You will need to examine each part of a story or passage in detail, looking at each word and sentence and drawing conclusions about the text as a whole. Here are some tips to help you.

Exercise 1

Look at a book that you have read, at home or in class. Think about it carefully using the headings in this section. Write these ideas down as brief notes.

> *Of Mice and Men* by John Steinbeck.
>
> Background – Two farmworkers travelling in America during the Depression.
>
> Summary – Main plot centres on George and Lennie's ambition to earn enough money to buy their own farm.
>
> Characters – George = small, clever; Lennie = huge, very strong ...

Background
You need to consider the setting of the book, in time and place. Where and when a story is set affects our understanding of it.

Genre
Does the text fit into a particular style or form of literature? Is it a romance, ghost story, thriller?

Summary
What is it about? Examine the main plot and any minor or subplots.

Characters
It is the characters who provide us with the action. From whose viewpoint is the story written? Does the author create a likeable or unpleasant character?

Language
Is the text shaped to suit people in general by being simple, direct and easy to read, or is it intended for a small readership?

Themes, messages and morals
There may be an underlying message in a text. Does the story make you think, or consider another point of view?

Criticism
It is quite acceptable to give your opinion on a book – providing you give good reason for your comments and provide evidence from the text to support them.

Exercise 2

Choose a character from a story you have enjoyed. Write notes for a character study of them. Think carefully about their appearance, personality and behaviour and their relationship with other characters. Explain why you chose this character. Use quotations from the book to support what you say about them.

Tactics
Look carefully at any text.

Learn the various reading skills and use them.

Practise close reading.

Studying persuasive texts

Every day of our lives we are subjected to persuasion of some sort. It could be in the form of advertising in newspapers and magazines, television and radio; through the post as junk mail; through the internet websites or email and over the telephone from telesales callers.

However, there are gentler and more subtle ways of influencing someone. The story that follows uses this 'soft' approach, although it has a powerful and important message. Read the story and think about both the moral or message, and the method the writer uses to get her point across before you move on to the explanation.

A Fable for Tomorrow

There was once a town in the heart of America where all life seemed to live in harmony with its surroundings. The town lay in the midst of a checkerboard of prosperous farms, with fields of grain and hillsides of orchards where… white clouds of bloom drifted above the green fields. In autumn, oak and maple and birch set up a blaze of colour that flamed and flickered across a backdrop of pines. Then foxes barked in the hills… half hidden in the mists of the autumn mornings.

Exercise 1

Either **1** Use the style of a fable or fairy story to write a warning tale of your own.

> Once there was a town with neat and tidy streets, and litter bins that were emptied regularly ...

Or **2** Rewrite a well-known fairy story in a modern way.

> Little Red Riding Hood was sick of her red cloak. Purple was in fashion ...

Along the roads, laurel, viburnum and alder, great ferns and wildflowers delighted the traveller's eye through much of the year. Even in winter the roadsides were places of beauty, where countless birds came to feed on the berries and on the seed heads of the dried weeds rising above the snow. The countryside was, in fact, famous for the abundance and variety of its bird life, and when the flood of migrants was pouring through in spring and autumn people travelled great distances to observe them. Others came to fish the streams, which flowed clear and cold out of the hills and contained shady pools where trout lay. So it had been from the days many years ago when the first settlers raised their houses, sank their wells, and built their barns.

Then a strange blight crept over the area and everything began to change. Some evil spell had settled on the community: mysterious maladies swept the flocks of chickens; the cattle and sheep sickened and died. Everywhere was a shadow of death. The farmers spoke of much illness among their families. In the town the doctors had become more and more puzzled by new kinds of sickness appearing among their patients. There had been several sudden and unexplained deaths, not only among adults but even among children, who would be stricken suddenly while at play and die within a few hours.

There was a strange stillness. The birds, for example – where had they gone? Many people spoke of them, puzzled and disturbed. The feeding stations in the backyard were deserted. The few birds seen anywhere were moribund; they trembled violently and could not fly… On the mornings that had once throbbed with the dawn chorus of robins, catbirds, doves, jays, wrens, and scores of other bird voices there was now no sound; only silence lay over the fields and woods and marsh.

On the farms the hens brooded, but no chicks hatched. The farmers complained that they were unable to raise any pigs – the litters were small and the young survived only a few days. The apple trees were coming into bloom but no bees droned among the blossoms, so there was no pollination and there would be no fruit…

In the gutters under the eaves and between the shingles of the roof, a white, granular powder still showed in a few patches; some weeks before it had fallen like snow upon the roofs and the lawns, the fields and the streams.

No witchcraft, no enemy action had silenced the rebirth of new life in this stricken world. The people had done it themselves.

From A Silent Spring by Rachel Carson

Exercise 2

Give five reasons why the extract from *A Silent Spring* is so effective.

> The ending is unexpected.

Exercise 3

Some stories have a message or moral. What do you thinks is the moral of *A Silent Spring*?

Tactics

Use descriptive writing to persuade and inform as well as to interest your reader.

Always think of the most suitable form in which to write.

37

Reading non-fiction

At home and school, you will encounter a great deal of non-fiction writing, be it a recipe in cookery, history and geography research, following instructions for a science experiment or understanding a concept in maths. To help you further, read the following extract.

The Story of Niagara Falls

The Niagara River has been cutting its way across the shelf of rock between Lake Ontario and Lake Erie for about 20 000 years. It seems a long time in terms of human experience, but compared to the 500 million year-old rocks of the Niagara Escarpment, Niagara Falls was born yesterday.

If we consider the rocks of the Escarpment to be one day old, the Niagara River as we know it has been in existence for only four seconds. Yet in this short space of time the river has cut seven miles of gorge and removed billions of tons of rock. The Niagara River is not only very young but, geologically speaking, it's working at breakneck speed.

Before we look closer at the last four seconds on our geological clock, let's go back a little further to 11:57pm. This corresponds to a period about a million years ago when much of North America was covered with ice. The glaciers advanced and receded several times as the earth's climate changed. At 11:59:56pm they finally disappeared. The depression left by the great weight of ice filled with water and became the forerunner of [the] present Great Lakes.

This fresh-water sea found many outlets to the Atlantic Ocean. One outlet spilled over the Niagara Escarpment at present-day Queenston and Niagara Falls was born.

Exercise 1

Find a recipe book, a set of rules for a sport or game or the instructions for a scientific experiment. Rewrite the instructions as simply and as clearly as you can. Use bullet points to show each stage or step.

- Each player needs a counter.
- Players take turns to throw the dice.

When the Niagara River began cascading over the 250 foot-high Escarpment, the pounding water quickly wore away the soft shale under the upper layer of limestone. As more shale washed away the limestone layer became increasingly unstable until finally it broke off. The Niagara River had taken its first bite into the Escarpement. The cycle was repeated again and again over the next several thousand years. The Falls crept gradually upstream.

From Niagara and the Daredevils *by Philip Mason*

Although the passage is not a difficult one, the skills you used to read it are quite advanced.

Title
In the example, it is obvious what the subject of the piece is going to be! But that is not always the case, sometimes you will need to look for clues in the title before you start reading.

Order
Some non-fiction writing (recipes, instructions and directions, for example) has a clear, logical and, possibly, numbered order. In the extract each paragraph is an individual unit telling us about some aspect of the formation of the Falls. The writer signals each change of subject with key words and phrases, such as *If we consider ...* , *Before ...* and *When ...* .

Meaning
As the writer makes each point it may be necessary for them to give an example or some explanation. This usually helps the reader by supporting and emphasising what has been said.

Language
Writing for different purposes and subjects requires a range of language styles and vocabulary. Sometimes unfamiliar scientific or technical terms are used. What do you do if you are puzzled by a word which you have never met before? If you have read the passage a couple of times you can look again at the word in context.

Exercise 2

Look up an entry in an encyclopedia for a person or a topic that has been covered in schools (the life of Shakespeare, for example). List, in note form, the ten most important facts you can find on that subject. You will need to read carefully. Only select the information which is most important.

- Shakespeare lived from 1564–1616.
- He was born and died in Stratford-upon-Avon.
- He spent most of his adult years in London.

Tactics
Practise your reading skills by looking at different types of non-fiction.

Watch out for clues, signals and key words which might help your understanding.

Studying poetry

Poetry is a way of expressing thoughts, feelings, ideas and experiences which would be inappropriate as a play or story. Poetry allows a writer to share experiences which have been important to them. They might do this in rhyme, by using a recognised form or pattern, or as free verse, using no pattern, rhythm or rhyme at all. Try to think of poetry as pictures or snapshots in which both simple and complicated ideas or stories can be communicated.

The following poem is by the American poet Robert Frost, and is about a time when he was faced with a decision.

The Road Not Taken

Two roads diverged in a yellow wood,
And sorry I could not travel both
And be one traveller, long I stood
And looked down one as far as I could
To where it bent in the undergrowth;   5

Then took the other, as just as fair,
And having perhaps the better claim,
Because it was grassy and wanted wear;
Though as for that the passing there
Had worn them really about the same,   10

And both that morning equally lay
In leaves no step had trodden black,
Oh, I kept the first for another day!
Yet knowing how way leads on to way,
I doubted if I should ever come back.   15

I shall be telling this with a sigh
Somewhere ages and ages hence:
Two roads diverged in a wood, and I –
I took the one less travelled by,
And that made all the difference.   20

Exercise 1

Use the bulleted list above to draft a brief explanation of the poem, its meaning and its impact. Include your own feelings about it.

> Meaning – The most obvious meaning of the poem is that the poet has reached a fork in a road. There is a deeper meaning though...

40

Always look carefully at each word in a poem – the poet has chosen them for a reason.   AL

One of the first things to remember when you read a poem is that the poet has usually worked and reworked the poem to produce a final version which reflects their ideas and feelings exactly. This redrafting process is one you will have been encouraged to use in your own writing.

There are several points you should think about when looking at a poem:

- The meaning of the poem
  Here the poet is speaking about the choice between two roads.
  He could have said that in a simple sentence. Instead, he writes a poem about it. Reading between the lines we might guess that the decision was an especially important one.

- How the title gives us a way into the poem
  The poem is called 'The Road Not Taken'. Again, we could read into this that the poet regrets the choice he made or is, perhaps, just curious about the other road. Why does he walk along the less popular path?

- The construction or form of the poem
  The poem is written in four verses, each having five lines. The rhyme scheme is *a, b, a, a, b*. The words are simple and straightforward – the poet does not let any unfamiliar words prevent him from getting his meaning across, even though some of the expressions might seem strange to us.

- Who the poet is speaking to
  Is the poet speaking to the reader or someone or something else?

- Your own opinion
  Remember that you are entitled to your own opinion about the poem, as long as you support what you say with evidence from the text itself.

Exercise 2

Think of a time when you made an important decision. Was it the right choice or was it a disaster? Write about it either as a short story or in a simple poem form.

Tactics

Which poetry forms do you know already? Look up and remember five of the more common ones, for example limerick, sonnet, riddle, haiku, ballad.

41

The front page

As a student in Year 9, you are probably more familiar with television and radio as news-carrying media, but it is important to learn about other forms of media. You will almost certainly be asked to present something in the form of a newspaper article at some time so here is some basic information.

Tabloids and broadsheets

Newspapers come in different sizes. The larger ones, or broadsheets, include *The Times*, *The Guardian* and *The Telegraph*, while the smaller ones (tabloids) are those like *The Daily Mail* and *The Sun*. Each paper caters for a different range of readers. A paper shapes the news to suit the people it believes are reading it and so may give a certain slant or bias to what it says.

Hitting the headlines

You have heard the expression 'headline news' – it simply means important news. (Bear in mind that what is a priority for a tabloid may not be for a broadsheet. Local papers will also focus on local rather than national stories.) The amount of space given to a headline varies, but the object is to make it eye-catching. A headline often uses humour in the form of puns, or word jokes. Headlines must attract a reader's interest enough to make them read on.

Exercise 1

Look at two different newspapers, a tabloid and a broadsheet. Compare the space given to:

1 headlines
2 text
3 pictures
4 adverts

Exercise 2

Collect and note down the most catchy and dramatic headlines you see in the next week.

> 'Bin men talk rubbish'   'New president is an alien'

What's it all about?
Having got your attention, the first paragraph of the article will outline the main points of the story. A tabloid newspaper will write this summary more briefly than a broadsheet.

Tell me more!
Having got the reader this far, the writer will use other skills and devices to keep you reading. For example, each paragraph leads the reader on to the next by using 'signposts', or words showing the order of events. Headings and subheadings are also used.

Tell me the truth!
Take care to note whether you are reading facts or opinions. Are you given accurate information – or the personal views of the writer or editor?
A reporter may also quote from an interview but use what is said out of context.
For example, an eyewitness may be quoted as saying, '*It was shocking!*' when what they said was, '*It was shocking at the time but I realise now it was nothing really.*'

Put me in the picture
Photographs, diagrams and illustrations all help to support a story; they are all types of 'evidence'.

Mind your language!
The style and tone of writing will vary from one paper to another and so will the choice of vocabulary. In general, tabloids tend to use simpler words and expressions and the articles are usually shorter. Broadsheet papers use a wider range of words and the news items need more thought and concentration to understand them.

Exercise 3

Design and draft a front page for a school, class or club paper. You could write this by hand in columns or you may have use of a computer and special software which will make the job easier.

Tactics

Learn how to summarise a story.

Notice how writers link paragraphs together.

Presentation in other forms

For thousands of years people have communicated with each other in some form of writing. Writing does not happen by accident. The writing which you see every day of your life, at home and at school, was written for a reason. The writer is usually clear about who is going to read what they have written. They will have thought about the purpose and the audience. Just as a writer has asked themselves, 'Why am I writing?' and, 'Who am I writing for?' you, as a reader, should be thinking in the same way. What makes a piece of writing so effective? What skills has the writer used?

Writers also make very deliberate choices about the best form to use. For example, it would be a mistake to explain some brief instructions in the form of a long story or to write about a serious matter using a postcard.

In the same way, writing varies in its formality or seriousness. If you used a casual and humorous tone in an examination you would give the wrong impression to the examiner. A letter to a friend or relative would be informal – a letter of complaint or apology to a stranger would be formal.

In the course of your life you will read a wide range of material – fiction and non-fiction, letters, essays, reports, poems, plays, newspapers and magazines. Most of the more common forms are looked at elsewhere in this book. Here we are going to look at one important form of reading which will be followed up later in the writing section.

Exercise 1

Using the skills of both research and advertising, design a web page to advertise your school, a club or other interest group. The task needs you to both inform and to influence your reader.

Reading for research

In the past you will have been asked to write a project or topic – perhaps for science, history or geography. By now you are familiar with the process, but in Year 9 you will know that it is not simply a case of copying out sections from a book. You will be expected to read, understand and question what you find. In Years 10 and 11 you will be asked to produce coursework for a range of subjects using these quite sophisticated skills.

Here are some general guidelines to help you assess these various forms:

- Purpose – How well does it inform?
- Audience – Is the intended audience wide and general or small and specific?
- Reliability – Is the source one which is well-informed and trustworthy?
- Up to date – Only ever use sources which are as recent as possible. An older text may not be accurate.
- Bias – Is the point of view one-sided or does the material give a balanced picture of the subject ?
- Fact and opinion – Make sure that any information is supported by evidence. An opinion might be interesting, but is it right?
- Range – In your research, have you found information from a variety of sources or have you kept to just one book?
- Selection of material – In research, it is not necessary to read every word. Use the skills of skimming and scanning to find relevant material.
- Recording – You will, of course, write down what you find out – but use your own words as far as possible. An article printed from the internet or a CD-ROM encyclopedia is not your own work. It is also important to make a note of where all your information comes from and to write this in the 'sources' section of your project.

Exercise 2

Look at some research that you have done recently for any school subject. Compare what you have done against the research checklist above (purpose, audience, etc.).

Which of these sources did you use?

> book   encyclopedias
>
> specialist/reference books
>
> newspapers and magazines
>
> internet   websites   email
>
> CD-ROMs   special software

Tactics

Remember to think of the purpose of and the audience for what you read.

Revise your use of sources in the library.

45

Reading Shakespeare

In preparation for the National Tests, in May of Year 9, you will study a Shakespeare play. Paper 2 will test your understanding of *one* section of *one* play.

Although you already know about Shakespeare and have looked at some of his work, for Paper 2 you must to study your chosen section, or sections, very carefully. So what can you do to make the job easier? Here are some ideas which will help you gain a better knowledge of any of the chosen plays:

Whole text
You could answer the questions in the test just by reading the section on its own – but you would probably not do very well! It is important to understand the section *in context*. You can do this in a number of ways:

- **Theatre**
  Many schools arrange a theatre trip so that you can see the play on stage. Make a point of going if you can. Drama workshops can also help.

- **Film**
  All of the chosen plays are available on video and sometimes as short cartoons.

- **Books**
  Visit your local and school library. You will find books explaining the main storyline of each play, for example *Lamb's Tales from Shakespeare*. There are also comic strip and cartoon forms available, as well as story tapes or audio plays which you can borrow.

Exercise 1

Once you are familiar with your chosen play, draw out the main events in a flow chart, list or timeline. Only include the most important things. Check your work against the text.

> Macbeth shows bravery in battle.
>
> Meets witches and hears three prophecies (Glamis, Cawdor, King).
>
> Made Thane of Cawdor ...

Exercise 2

Make a storyboard for one of your sections. Using A3 paper, sketch out the scene in no more than ten frames. This can be done as a cartoon or stick men – with speech bubbles.

- **Act I**

  The first act of any Shakespeare play contains the most important information – it sets the scene for what comes next. If you take some trouble understanding this, the sequence of the play will be much easier to follow.

- **Themes**

  Within any Shakespeare play you will find themes or subjects which make you think. In *Macbeth* and *Julius Caesar* for instance, there are themes such as 'ambition' and 'jealousy'.

- **Characters**

  Notice how the characters in a play behave towards each other and especially how they speak in different situations. Think about how the characters change over the course of the play. How does Shakespeare encourage his audience to like or dislike certain characters?

Sentence level

Although Shakespeare does use what you might think of as sentences in his plays most of them are written in blank verse. This is verse that does not usually rhyme. Each line has a pattern of ten syllables. The syllables are in pairs – the first syllable is a weak beat and the second a strong one. Five groups of pairs in each line gives what is called iambic pentameter and gives a rhythm. For example, Friar Laurence: What early tongue so sweet saluteth me? di dum/di dum/di dum/di dum/di dum.

Word level

Shakespeare wrote his plays four hundred years ago and during that time the English language has changed. Some words are no longer used and others have a new and different meaning. The main message or meaning of a speech, however, should still be fairly clear. Do not worry if you do not understand every word.

You will notice that the grammar is also different. Words may be contracted or shortened in an unusual way.

Exercise 3

Chose a character who appears in one of your sections. Find and write down five quotations which you feel describe them most accurately or tell you something special about them.

> Romeo says that Juliet *doth teach the torches to burn bright.*

Exercise 4

Look at one of the scenes you are studying and find out the meaning of five of the more unusual or difficult words.

> Twelfth Night *usurp* = to remove

Tactics

Read the play aloud.

Try to understand the tone of voice of each character.

Reading in paper 1 (1)

In the first part of Paper 1 for the National Tests you will be asked to look at a piece of personal writing which might be part of a fiction story or an extract from an autobiography. You will be expected to read it with understanding and show that you are able to notice important features which the author has used.

Read the extract twice. In your first reading make sure that you have a general understanding of the main events and characters in the passage. In your second reading, look out for the ways in which the author has made the story amusing, entertaining or more lifelike.

The Schoolroom

Each morning was war without declaration; no one knew who would catch it next. We stood to attention, half-crippled in our desks, till Miss B walked in, whacked the walls with a ruler, and fixed us with her squinting eye. "Good a-morning, children!" "Good morning, Teacher!" The greeting was like a rattling of swords...

So we did not much approve of Crabby – though she was responsible for our excellent reflexes. Apart from this, her teaching was not memorable. She appears in my recollection as merely a militant figure, a hunched-up little creature all spring-coils and slaps – not a monster by any means, but a natural manifestation of what we expected of school.

For school in my day, that day, Crabby's day, seemed to be designed simply to keep us out of the air and from following the normal pursuits of the fields...

And indeed, there came the inevitable day when rebellion raised its standard; when the tension was broken and a hero emerged whom we would willingly have named streets after... though we gave little support at the time.

Spadge Hopkins it was, and I must say we were surprised. He was one of those heavy, full-grown boys, thick-legged, red-fisted, bursting with flesh, designed for the great out-doors. He was nearly fourteen by then, and physically out of scale – at least as far as our school was concerned.

Exercise 1

In your own words, explain what the following expressions might mean.

1 half crippled in our desks – Gives the impression of children trapped in their old-fashioned desks, quite unable to move.
2 squinting eye
3 a rattling of swords
4 like a bullock in ballet shoes
5 Crabby sprung like a yellow cat

Tactics

Revise metaphor, simile and alliteration.

The sight of him squeezed into his tiny desk was worse than a bullock in ballet-shoes. He wasn't much of a scholar; he groaned as he worked, or hacked at his desk with a jack-knife. Miss B took her pleasure in goading him, in forcing him to read aloud; or asking him sudden unintelligible questions which made him flush and stumble.

The great day came... Crabby B was at her sourest and Spadge Hopkins had had enough. He began to writhe in his desk, and roll his eyes, and kick with his boots, and mutter: "She'd better look out – 'er – Crabby B. She'd better, that's all. I can tell you... "

We didn't quite know what the matter was, in spite of his meaning looks. Then he threw down his pen, and said, "--- it all," got up and walked to the door.

"And where are you going, young man, may I ask?" said Crabby with her awful leer.

Spadge paused and looked her straight in the eye.

"If it's any business of yourn."

We shivered with pleasure at this defiance. Spadge leisurely made for the door.

"Sit down this instant!" Crabby suddenly screamed. "I won't have it!"

"Ta-ta," said Spadge.

Then Crabby sprung like a yellow cat, spitting and clawing with rage. There was a shameful moment of heavy breathing and scruffling while the teacher tore at his clothes. Spadge caught her hands in his great fists and held her at arms length, struggling.

"Come and help me, someone!" wailed Crabby, demented. But nobody moved; we just watched. We saw Spadge lift her up and place her on the top of the cupboard, then walk out of the door and away. There was a moment's silence, then we all laid down our pens and began to stamp the floor in unison. Crabby stayed where she was, on top of the cupboard, drumming her heels and weeping.

From Cider with Rosie *by Laurie Lee*

Laurie Lee writes with some affection and humour about what appears to be a true incident from his childhood. There is a rich use of vocabulary and 'trigger' words. These call for a reaction from the reader and attempt to make the writing more interesting.

Exercise 2

Imagine that you are Spadge Hopkins. Briefly tell the story from your point of view.

> Day after day I went to that school and day after day it was the same. Always nagging, always moaning – always crabby. That's why we call her Old Crabby. Why coudn't she just leave me be? But that day I'd had enough . . .

Reading in paper 1 (2)

In the second part of Paper 1 you will be asked to look at a non-fiction piece. There is a broad range of things you may be asked to read – from factual extracts from books, biographies, entries from reference books, brochures and scientific or technical writing. You may even be asked to read a poem.

The intention here is to test whether you can read and understand forms of writing other than fiction (stories). The writing may be factual, but it might also be literary or non-literary. You will need to read carefully and find different pieces of information (some of them may not be obvious) and you may be asked to change information into another form.

Read the extract below and think about it before you try the exercises.

The Greatest was Blondin

Jean Francois Gravelet, the great Blondin, was the first of many tightrope walkers to appear at Niagara Falls. In spite of his imitators – some of whom performed stunts that equalled or even surpassed those of Blondin – the fame and the glory remained Blondin's. No other stunter before or since ever came close to achieving his success.

Blondin was no idle boaster. On June 30, 1859 the rope was in position and at five o'clock in the afternoon Blondin started the trip that was to make history. He moved cautiously down the rope toward the centre of the gorge. To steady himself he carried at 40-foot long balancing pole. Blondin was too good a showman to make the trip appear easy. His hesitations and swayings began to build a tension that soon had the huge crowd gripped in suspense. The descending section of the rope was steadied by guys carried back to the shore line, but Blondin now

---

Exercise 1

Imagine that you were there on the day of Blondin's attempt to cross Niagara Falls on a tightrope and write your own eyewitness account. This will be *personal* writing, so you can express your feelings and opinions as well as the facts of what you saw.

> I was very excited about my invitation to see Blondin's attempt to cross Niagara Falls...

approached the unsupported centre section. He edged his way along the centre of the rope. He paused, swaying and balancing. It was David and Goliath magnified one hundred times. It seemed incredible that this tiny figure on a slender, almost invisible thread could so defy the mighty Niagara. Incredulous watchers saw him lower a rope to the Maid of the Mist, pull up a bottle and sit down while he refreshed himself.

There were plenty of parched throats in the crowd, but no one dared take their eyes from Blondin for a second.

At last he began the ascent toward the Canadian shore. But he was not finished yet. Near the shore he paused, steadied the balancing pole and suddenly executed a back somersault. Men screamed, women fainted. Those near the rope wept and begged him to come in.

When he finally stepped off the rope he was grabbed by a delirious, shouting, crying, sobbing horde of well-wishers who escorted him to a champagne reception. It had been the stunt of the century. Nothing could surpass it and only one man would equal it – Blondin. For 18 minutes he had held the crowd on the knife edge of suspense. Fortified with champagne, he announced that he would return the same way he had come. To thundering cheers Blondin skipped and gambolled his way back across the river in less than seven minutes. It was a day long remembered at Niagara Falls.

From Niagara and the Daredevils by Philip Mason

Exercise 2

Write a front page newspaper story describing Blondin's crossing. As a reporter your writing should be *impersonal*, but you might still use personal, eyewitness accounts (like the one in Exercise 1) or interviews with people on the spot.

Tactics

Become familiar with as many different forms of non-fiction writing as you can.

Learn to 'read between the lines'.

This morning a large crowd saw Jean Francois Gravelet, the great Blondin, successfully cross Niagara Falls on a tightrope.

3

Reading checklist

Reading is an essential skill; it would be difficult to survive successfully in modern life without it, so here is some general guidance to help you.

● ## Wide reading

Try to get as broad an experience of as many different forms of writing as you can. This will help you in the National Tests in Year 9 and in English and other subjects in Years 10 and 11.

Reading strategies

First, use any way you can to extend your knowledge and experience. Visit libraries, browse in bookshops and ask friends and family to recommend books. Second, use the skills of skimming, scanning and close reading when you are asked to study a text.

Forms

Writing comes in many different forms and it is important to become familiar with them.

Purpose and audience

Ask yourself two questions: 'What is the writer's aim?' and 'Who are they writing for?'

Fact and opinion

It is important to know the difference between a fact (which should have evidence to support it) and an opinion (a personal view or feeling).

Language

Use your skills to study any writing at word, sentence and whole text level. How well does the structure and vocabulary suit the task in hand?

Genre

Fiction is often written in a particular style. A story might be a romance, thriller or adventure – or contain elements of several types of writing. Try to notice the main features of the more common ones.

Context

Looking at a piece of writing in context means to think about when and where it was written. The time and place in which a writer lives, together with their the culture and background, will influence their writing.

Setting

This means when and where the story itself was set. Do not confuse this with the last point. You could write a story in the context of the twenty–first century (you are living here and now) but set your story in the future and in outer space.

Reading between the lines

Writers do not always make their meaning clear. Sometimes this is done deliberately to make the reader think. For example, if someone wrote *He sat down heavily in the chair with a sigh* they could simply have said *He was fed up*. The first sentence gives an effective image; the second is dull.

Strategies for writing

Planning and drafting

It has been said that genius is 10% inspiration and 90% perspiration! It is impossible to do anything well without effort. The same is true of any writing task. The only difference is that 80% of your time should be 'thinking time' and 20% 'writing time'. The 'thinking time' should include your planning and drafting.

When a task is set, anyone who begins writing straightaway is not making the best use of their time. Your object is to write well – not write quickly. Even in an examination situation, planning will pay off.

You will already be familiar with various ways of putting your ideas together. Here are some you may know:

Stage 1

- brainstorming, lists and notes
- timeline
- mind map
- topic web or spider diagram
- flow chart

Exercise 1

Use one of the Stage 1 methods to help you think about a character in the Shakespeare play you are studying, a character in a book you have read or as preparation for your next writing task.

> Romeo attends the ball in disguise. Sees Juliet and falls in love ...

Different methods suit different tasks. Brainstorming is a useful way of exploring a wide range of ideas – you may not use all of the ideas, but at least you will have considered them. Flow charts and timelines are helpful when the events that you wish to write about happen in a particular order or in sequence. Topic webs and spider diagrams enable you to get your thoughts on paper – but you still need to decide which idea is to form the first (introductory) paragraph and which one would make a good conclusion.

Stage 2

The next step is to put the thoughts and ideas in order. It is not necessary, or appropriate sometimes, to keep to the order in which events happen. By numbering each note, you can see what comes next. This is not the final draft so there is still the opportunity to change what has been written.

Stage 3

Hopefully, you will still be prepared to alter things, adding relevant ideas and information as you go along.

When you are satisfied that you have answered the question, drafted and redrafted your work (edited and proofread) you will be ready to hand in a piece you can be proud of.

Exercise 2

Having drafted and checked your work, you are ready to write the final draft. We could think of this as the third stage. Write up your work from Exercise 1, making sure that you do a final check and that your writing is clear and easy to follow.

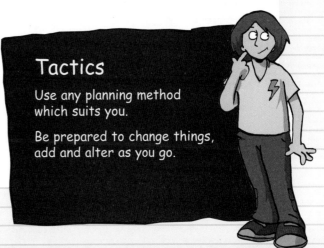

Tactics

Use any planning method which suits you.

Be prepared to change things, add and alter as you go.

Writing poetry

With any creative activity, whether it is painting or pottery, writing or sculpture, getting started is always the hard part. It is the same with poetry. What are you going to write about? Should it rhyme? Will your poem need to follow a set form or pattern? All these questions can be difficult to answer.

When you were younger you may have been asked to write an acrostic. This is a simple way to get you writing – it uses what you already know and gives you some confidence. But the end result is not always very good! That is because it is difficult to be really creative and original using a rigid structure.

But there are other, similar ideas that you can use to help you write poetry. By using a framework, but not keeping quite so strictly to it, you will find that you can write some effective and successful poetry.

Read the poem below through twice. Think about it for a few moments before reading on.

Leopard

Gentle hunter
his tail plays on the ground
While he crushes the skull.

Beautiful death
Who puts on a spotted robe
When he goes to his victim.

Playful killer
Whose loving embrace
Splits the antelope's heart.

From the Yoruba, translated by Ulli Beier

Exercise 1

Use the framework on page 57 to write a poem of your own on a different subject. You may like to choose another creature – or instead, use the three steps to describe a character or experience.

Sleek, soft and silky
Gleaming tortoiseshell fur ball ...

This short poem has three verses, each with three lines. It has no rhythm or rhyme. The leopard is portrayed as a beautiful and effective killer.

In the past you will have come across the haiku; these are three-line poems with five syllables in the first line, seven in the second and five in the third. Although this makes a total of 17 syllables, very often (because of the difficulty of translating them from the Japanese original) they may have 21 or more. We will use the structure of the haiku as the basis for the following poetry framework:

Step 1   Choose a creature which interests you and which you know about – it might be a mammal, fish or insect; wild or domestic. Write a haiku describing its appearance. Do not worry too much if you use more than 17 syllables. If a word is important, use it.

Step 2   Write some more haiku which look at other aspects of the creature, for example: How does it move, eat or hunt? How does it behave? What does it like or dislike? This process should give you at least another four haiku.

Step 3   Rearrange and alter your haiku in any way you wish. You could add extra lines, words or syllables. You could change the order or put all the lines together to make a single verse of 12 or 15 lines. You might decide to include alliteration, similes or metaphors.

Exercise 2

1   If you are feeling confident, try other forms based on the use of syllables, for example cinquains (a five-line stanza) and clerihews (a comic verse of two couplets of metrically irregular lines and containing the name of a famous person).
2   Try copying the style of rhyming forms like limericks and sonnets.
3   Write your own lyrics to a popular song.

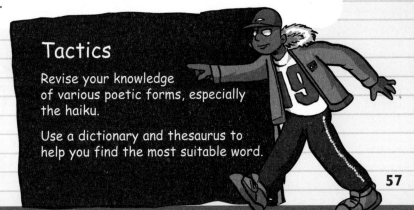

Tactics

Revise your knowledge of various poetic forms, especially the haiku.

Use a dictionary and thesaurus to help you find the most suitable word.

RED ALERT RED ALERT RED ALERT RED

Writing a script

Writing takes three main forms. It is either *prose* (writing in sentences and paragraphs, like stories, reports or instructions), *poetry* (haiku, sonnets or ballads and so on) or a *play*.

Plays are written in acts, which are then divided into scenes. A play might have five acts, each with one or more scenes. It is also possible to find one-act plays. If you have started to look at your chosen Shakespeare play or have taken part in a play, you will be familiar with the layout. Plays are meant to be performed, so a script gives the exact words that a character must say. This is done by giving the character's name and their part – written without any speech marks.

There is also other information provided to tell the actors how a speech should be delivered and to tell them how and where to move. A script also indicates where the play takes place and may give information about the set, costume, sound and lighting for the play. All this is usually written in italics and is called the narration. The narrator's words are not spoken.

Read the following extract from *Romeo and Juliet*. Even if you do not know the play well or it is not your selected play, you can probably guess how the words might be spoken and assume something about the characters' actions and expressions. Romeo and Juliet have just met and have fallen in love immediately.

Exercise 1

Write a script for an unscripted/improvised play from drama or English. Photocopy the parts. Rehearse and perform the play in a group.

Romeo: (to Juliet)	If I profane with my unworthiest hand This holy shrine, the gentle sin is this, My lips, two blushing pilgrims, ready stand To smooth that rough touch with a single kiss.
Juliet:	Good pilgrim, you do wrong your hand too much, Which mannerly devotion shows in this, For saints have hands that pilgrims' hands do touch, And palm to palm is holy palmers' kiss.
Romeo:	Have not saints lips and holy palmers too?
Juliet:	Ay, pilgrim, lips that they must use in prayer.
Romeo:	O then, dear saint, let lips do what hands do: They pray, grant thou, lest faith turn to despair.
Juliet:	Saints do not move, though grant for prayers' sake.
Romeo:	Then move not while my prayer's effect I take Thus from my lips, by thine, my sin is purged. (Kissing her.)
Juliet:	Then have my lips the sin that they have took.
Romeo:	Sin from my lips? O trepass sweetly urged! Give me my sin again. (Kissing her again.)
Juliet	You kiss by th' book.

Exercise 2

1 Create a script using part of your chosen Shakespeare play as a basis. Put the parts into modern language – do not use the original words. (You will notice that the play will sound very different, even dull, using modern expression.)
2 Choose people from your class to play the various parts.
3 Design a modern set and use up-to-date costumes.
4 Perform your play in class.

Tactics

Do *not* use speech marks.

Do include helpful direction for the actors.

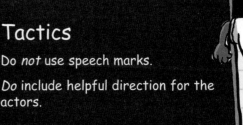

RED ALERT RED ALERT RED ALERT RE

Imaginative and narrative writing

Imaginative writing is one of the most difficult forms to do well. Students either let their imaginations run riot and produce work without much structure or they lack the ideas to get started. Having a vivid imagination is a wonderful gift – but, uncontrolled, it can become a monster. On the other hand, it is understandable that being faced with writing a story from your imagination can seem like an overwhelming task.

To put your mind at rest, tests and examinations these days rarely ask you to write just from your imagination! (Imaginative work demands too much time and will probably be set as work to do in class or at home instead.)

Imaginative work has a story or narrative. But the sort of narrative writing that you will do is more likely to be based on your own experiences. Writing about what you know generally produces better work. Whether your writing is from your imagination or from real life, there are some points which you need to consider.

Planning

By now you understand the importance of planning and will not need reminding. With imaginative and narrative work it is, if anything, even more important than usual. Having brainstormed your ideas, it is essential that you have a clear picture of the order of events. Your aim in writing, whether to amuse or amaze, shock or puzzle your reader, should also be clear in your mind. If you are writing in a particular genre (a set type of story – thriller, adventure or romance and so on) this will affect your eventual choice of language and expression. Follow up your brainstorm by jotting down two or three plot ideas using the

Exercise 1

Think about writing in a particular genre (fantasy, mystery, science-fiction, supernatural, thriller or adventure). Brainstorm your ideas and then write down three plots which you could use.

> Fantasy story. Schoolgirl who is bullied – gains magical powers. Overcomes the bullies and helps other victims.

Exercise 2

Think about some real experiences which have happened to you. Jot down a plan for a piece of writing. (You might choose a journey or holiday, an event from your past or some other memorable experience.)

> Butlins with grandparents and auntie – went out with auntie – got lost – Redcoat found me – found grandma and auntie in ballroom.

headings of 'Setting' (time and place), 'Events' (beginning, middle and end) and 'Characters'. The examples shown below are from the planning for a ghost/mystery story.

> Example
>
> Plot 1
> Setting (time/place) - 19th century. English countryside.
> Beginning 1. Servant girl - becomes pregnant.
> 2. Commits suicide - buried in an unmarked grave.
> 3. Grave always has flowers on it. Who puts them there?
> 4. End - Rich landowner discovered as father of baby. Feels guilty and puts flowers on the grave.
> Characters   - poor servant girl in love with
>   - rich young man

> Example
>
> Plot 2 Setting (time/place) - Medieval England. Site of monastery.
> Beginning 1. Strange sighting of ghost of monk.
> 2. Other strange happenings - things moving/missing.
> 3. Monastery records reveal history of monk murdered by local character? Why?
> 4. Monk and murderer rivals in love with same girl in their youth. (Still enemies even when one goes to the monastery.) Girl married someone else.
> 5. End - Monk killed in fight.
> Characters   - monk   - murderer   - girl   - future husband

Exercise 3

Interview an older relative about their life and experiences. Write up their life history.

Exercise 4

Use a notebook to write down storylines to use when you are asked to write in an imaginative way. You might find ideas on the news, in films or from real life.

Tactics

Try writing from your own experience if possible.

Think about your reader. What is your writing trying to do for them?

Descriptive writing

You will already be familiar with the task of creative writing. You should have completed work examining ways of beginning and ending stories and creative pieces; you know how to use paragraphs and key sentences. Read the following extract. (It might help you to jot down expressions that particularly impress you.)

A Windy Day

It was the sort of day that makes you feel glad to be indoors. The coal fire was burning quickly and the sash windows were rattling like a lid on a pot of boiling potatoes. The thunder-like roar in the throat of the chimney; the high-pitched buzz of the insulating tape on the front door frame; the scratching of thorn against glass on the patio: all these seemed to break the comparative silence inside the house.

I would have stayed indoors if it was possible, but I had agreed to call for an important friend and could not let her down. I got up from the sofa and switched off the television; staying in had made me feel lethargic and, although it was about 11 o'clock, sleep had barely been driven from my eyes ...

I went into my bedroom and threw myself onto the bed, switched on my CD player and lay wondering whether I should ring her and tell her I was ill or something of the sort.

Through my window I noticed a bird, probably a finch, perched on a violently swaying plum tree. Each time the bough moved, the bird leaned in the opposite direction, trying to compensate for the movement and retain its foothold on the bough. Alas, the wind was too strong; he fell off the bough and started to fly

Exercise 1

Replace the words and phrases italics to make these sentences more interesting.

1 We had a *nice* picnic the other day.
   We had a tremendous picnic the other day.
2 He told me to *get out of* the room.
3 I had *great* feeling when I finished first.
4 *At the end of the day*, we would all like to win the lottery.
5 What a *lovely* bouquet the bride carried!

into the wind, struggling against the turbulent air, barely moving. Realising the futility of its efforts, it turned to fly with the wind and was swept away at great speed and out of sight in mere seconds ...

I took my time to get ready but, overcoming my reluctance, I was soon wheeling my racing bike out of the garage. Ten minutes later I had only reached nearby Newport. People were walking around with strange, squinting expressions with tears in their eyes from airborne grit. Crisp wrappers were being whipped into a whirling frenzy, faster and faster and then, suddenly, falling to the ground.

The wind was now at least Force 6 or 7. Oaks swayed like blades of grass. Through the roar of the wind, I could hear a squeaking noise as the sign blew from side to side at the Chequers Inn. It hung at forty-five degrees, as if held by a string. The road seemed to cling to the wheels of my bike. It felt as though I was riding with the brakes on. All the time there was a tremendous roar in my ears; only when I turned my head to the side was there any respite from thunderous noise.

On arrival at my friend's house, I could see in the glass of the front door that my hair was all spiked up. I brushed it down as best I could.

I rang the doorbell.

I rang the doorbell again and after what seemed several minutes the door was flung open and my friend said,

"You took your time, didn't you?"

Non-fiction? Fiction? Fact?

Writers who *base* their writings on actual events, are writers of *non-fiction*. Writing that deals in *completely new* storylines is said to be fiction. (Even so, it is virtually impossible to write anything that is totally original.) Factual writing is the relating of 'true' facts – as in a scientific textbook or encyclopedia.

Exercise 2

Write a piece of descriptive writing of your own. Avoid over-used words, or clichés as they are called. Choose a subject that you know something about. Keep it simple. Make use of all the senses – sight, touch, taste and hearing.

The day began predictably enough until I reached the bus stop. There was the bus ready and waiting. It had broken down. I was going to be late and that meant trouble ...

Tactics

Use your senses in descriptive writing.

Avoid tired words or clichés.

63

Persuasive and argumentative writing

The ability to argue a point is important. Whether it is used to convince a friend that a particular opinion is right, to persuade someone to take a particular course of action or to make a strong case for or against something – this is an essential skill. You will need it in your English lessons during discussion work and in many of your other subjects, when answering essay and examination questions. Here are some points to bear in mind.

Think about the problem and the 'best' end result

Look carefully at the question, statement or problem before you write anything. Do not just jump in without thinking first. Your initial feelings about a subject may not be right. Be prepared to change your mind. Consider what final answer or outcome most accurately reflects the available evidence.

Collect your evidence

Your research may need to be quite wide – depending on the demands of the task. Where are you going to find your information?

- Books   You may be given some background information but will almost certainly need to try other sources, for example textbooks, library books, brochures and so on.
- People   For some pieces of work the opinions of other people, 'experts', clubs and societies may be helpful.

Exercise 1

1   Think about the argument for and against homework. Fold a piece of A4 paper in half lengthways. On the left-hand side note down the arguments *for* and on the right jot down the case *against*.
2   Using your notes to help you, research the views of your friends, family and teachers on the subject. Make sure that you get a fair cross-section of opinions.
3   Add the new evidence to your notes. Review your own opinion of the subject.

- The media   Newspapers, magazines, television, radio and other, up-to-date sources may be relevant.
- Technology   The internet, websites and web pages, CD-Roms and email may all provide you with answers to your problem.

Having found your information, you need to collect it together or *collate* it.

Think about the evidence
At this point you need to go back to the original question or task instructions. Think carefully about what you have found out. Balance the evidence against your own thoughts and feelings. Do you still hold the same opinion or opinions that you had at the start?

Presenting your material
As with any written work you will need to plan and draft your work. As you structure it, think all the time of what the opposite view might be. Is there a large amount of evidence both for and against? You will need to show that you have thought about both sides. It may even be necessary to leave the conclusion open-ended if there is no convincing, final answer. By arranging your evidence in brief, note form on each side (for and against) you may see the strongest case emerging.

Make sure that any statement you make is supported by evidence and followed up with further explanation. This, because of its three stages, is referred to as the 'hamburger method'.

statement

evidence/quotation

development

Exercise 2

Choose a character from either a Shakespeare play or a book which you have read and enjoyed. Using the guidelines above to help you, make the case that this character is vital to the play or book. Include quotations to support what you say!

The character of Bottom in
A Midsummer Night's Dream.

Bottom is important to the plot of the play because he links the real world of the Athenian workers and the supernatural world of the fairies. He also provides much of the humour ...

Tactics
Always use reliable sources.
Try the 'hamburger method'.

65

RED ALERT RED ALERT RED ALERT RED

Presentation of ideas

Earlier we looked at the skills necessary to read research material in a critical way. Here we will consider writing up your research.

Presenting projects and topics

Once you have completed your research you will need to sift through your material to see what is relevant and what should be discarded. This, together with structuring and presenting your work, is probably the most difficult task you will do. Here are some guidelines to help.

Cover and title page

These should be neat and clear. If you use an illustration for the cover, make sure that it is relevant to the project – but do not spend more time on that than you do on the writing itself!

Contents list

You owe it to your reader to guide them through the project. Just as paragraphs signpost the route through a piece of writing, number the pages so that your reader can follow your line of enquiry.

Introduction

Begin by saying simply and briefly what you have done and why.

Main content

Your chapters, sections, headings and subheadings should be clearly labelled. One chapter should lead on to the next in a logical fashion.

Exercise 1

Check a piece of research work which you have done against the guidelines above. (The work could be for any subject.) Have you covered all the main headings? What areas did you miss out? Was there anything that you could have done in a better way?

RED ALERT   *In any writing think of purpose and audience.*   A

Conclusion

Finish by referring back to the project. (In later years this section will be extremely important because it will reflect your findings, perhaps for some serious, examination level coursework or subject investigation.)

Sources

You will have used information from many sources – you must say what they were. This sometimes comes under the heading of 'References' or, if only books are used, 'Bibliography'.

Illustration

Depending on the subject and nature of the project, it may be important to include diagrams, graphs, sketches and photographs.

Glossary

This is like a dictionary. It usually contains special terms or words used in the project.

Index

Arrange the main subjects in alphabetical order and indicate which page they can be found on.

Appendix

This contains information which is referred to in the project but is not included in the main text or chapters. It may contain tables, charts or other additional material.

Acknowledgements

If someone has helped you, this is where you can thank them.

Presentation

Finally, check that your work is neat, clear and accurate.

Exercise 2

Draft a glossary (Jargon Buster) of your own. It could be for a school subject, or a hobby or interest of your own. Remember to put the entries in alphabetical order with a brief but clear explanation of what each one means. Look at the Jargon Buster in this book to give you the right idea.

Tactics

Revise the different forms of writing.

Look back at the section 'Presentation in other forms'.

RED ALERT RED ALERT RED ALERT RED

Letters and diaries

Personal writing takes a number of forms. You might retell a story from your own point of view – in which case the narrative would be a personal one. In the same way, if you were to write your autobiography, that would be personal writing too. Although any writing you do will contain your own views, ideas and opinions, these ideas may not always be as obvious as they are in 'personal' writing forms.

Writing of this type tends to be less formal than, say, an essay, report or comprehension answer although it still needs to be well-organised.

Personal letters

Personal letters are those sent to a friend or relative and are more casual in tone than a business letter. A formal business letter should be short, direct and to the point – your object could be to inform, demand or complain. In a personal letter you should try to make your writing interesting to the recipient; shape what you say to suit them.

The layout for both types of writing are similar – but with a business letter you would include both your address and theirs, and end *Yours faithfully* (or *Yours sincerely* if you know or have met the person). In neither style of letter should you put your name above your address – that always comes at the end.

Exercise 1

Write a letter to a friend or relative who you have not seen for some time.

Diaries

Unlike letters (business or personal), which communicate with other people, diaries are usually only seen by the writer. They are very private forms of writing which record personal thoughts, feelings and experiences. Some diaries have been read by other people, for example the writings of Samuel Pepys and Anne Frank. Diaries are often a useful way of remembering past events. You may also be asked to write the diary of a character in a book or play to show that you understand their actions and behaviour.

Remember these features when writing a diary:

*   Diaries record day to day events and observations, but try also to include those things that are different, unusual or special.
*   If the diary is private, you might use words and phrases, a code, or even your own form of shorthand – but remember, you need to be able to read it later!
*   A diary written as if you were a character (real or imaginary) must look at the detail of that character's life but still focus on any extraordinary events as well.
*   Diaries may also contain the hopes, dreams or ambitions of the writer.

Exercise 2

Write the diary for either yourself or for a character from a book, play or film. You could call it 'A week in the life of ...'

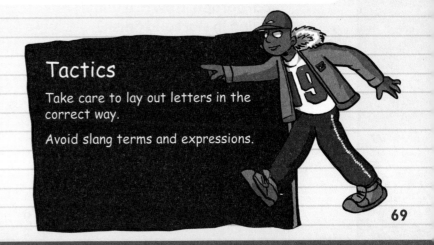

Tactics

Take care to lay out letters in the correct way.

Avoid slang terms and expressions.

69

RED ALERT RED ALERT RED ALERT RED

4

Writing checklist

Whether it is in your day-to-day work or what you do in the Tests, your writing is going to be assessed – and it is important to get it right. In Year 9 (as in Years 10 and 11) you are either writing for a teacher you know or for the examiner, who is a total stranger. It is vital that you check your work! Here are some guidelines to help you.

Before writing:

- look at your last few pieces of work. Read any comments that were made by your teacher and take special note of any mistakes.

- prepare your equipment – pens, notebooks, research resources, and so on.

- read the task instructions or essay/composition titles carefully.

- plan your work. Brainstorm ideas, then put your ideas in a topic web, spider diagram, flow chart or mind map. Think about, and jot down, what you want to say in each paragraph. How are you going to start and finish?

- look up any special words you are going to use.

- consider whether you need to find out any further information. Where will you find it?

After writing, check:

- your layout. How should the work be presented? Is it homework or classwork? Does it need a title or date? Does the layout fit the requirements of the task? For example, if you were asked to write a newspaper article, is it presented in that form?

- the content. What have you said? Is it interesting? Is it long enough?

- any expressions. Could you have said things in a better way?

- your vocabulary. Could you have used more suitable or effective words?

- the spellings. Did you use a dictionary? Did you use a spellcheck?

- the punctuation. Have you used full stops, commas and capital letters?

- your structure. Are your paragraphs clear? Does one subject lead on to another in an obvious and easy way?

- the presentation. Is your work clear and neat?

After marking, consider:

- whether your work grade got better.

- any comments your teacher made.

- whether your work is improving.

- what aspects of the checklist you are not very good at.

- how you could improve.

- whether you need help from your teacher.

5

Getting top marks

In the examination

Before you open the examination paper, make yourself comfortable. If your chair or table rocks, if the sun is in your eyes, or if there is a distraction of any sort, ask the invigilator to do something about it. You will not do your best when you are bothered by something, however slight.

Reading the examination paper

- The front cover of the paper will give you the instructions you need. These are known as the rubric. Do exactly what it tells you to do.

- Examiners really want you to do your best, so the paper is structured to give you the best possible chance. The rubric is intended to enable you to know exactly what you should be doing!

- Follow the time allocation carefully. If you are told to spend 10 minutes on question 1 and 35 minutes on question 4, it is because question 4 carries many more marks.

- Use all the time. The chances are that if you finish very early you have missed something important, so go back over your paper when you have done.

Studying the questions

Paper 1: Sections A and B

- Read the *italicised introduction* to each of the passage, the part that begins: 'This passage is ...' You are given the information to help you make sense of the passage.

- Each question contains the same advice: 'Refer to words and phrases in the passage to support your idea'. In other words, use quotations.

- The bullet points in the question tell you 'what you should comment on': use these points as separate paragraphs in your response.

- Do not stop writing an answer because you are at the bottom of a page. Carry on, even if for only one word.

Paper 1: Section C

- You have a choice of three essay titles. One might seem easier than the others, but all carry the same marks. Take the easy title – two-thirds of all candidates will think that is the hardest one; everyone has different likes and dislikes.

- 4a) generally calls for a story which you should avoid if you are no good at telling them!

  4b) gives you the chance to do descriptive or personal writing. People always write best from their own experience and the more dramatic the experience, the better the writing;

  4c) is the chance for argumentative writing and it refers back to the passage you have read in Section B. Do use quotations from Section B if you make this choice.

After the examination

- Don't listen to other people who tell you how well or how badly they have done.

- If you thought the paper was difficult, it is probably a good sign since you were answering the right questions.

- Celebrate!

73

Hotseating

The most important work you will be doing in Literature is studying a Shakespeare play ready for answering questions in the National Tests. A play has not been written to be read but to be acted so, if you can, try and see a production of your play either on stage or TV. This is not always possible, however, but there is no reason why you cannot participate in oral activities related to the play. And one of the most enjoyable and profitable ways of learning about the characters and themes is hotseating.

Hotseating

This is where you pretend to be a character from the play and answer questions from your fellow-students as if you are that person. In this way, you can explore the way the character thinks and the motivation behind the actions.

Exercise 1

Macbeth

Lady Macbeth meets her husband just before he kills Duncan. You are Lady Macbeth.
- Whose idea was it to kill Duncan?
- How does your husband feel about murdering him?
- Why might Duncan not suspect you want him dead?
- When your husband says he does not want to kill him, how do you react?
- How do you persuade him to do it?
- What is your plan for successfully murdering him?
- Why did you not kill him yourself?

Answer this question on the scene: 'What do you learn about Lady Macbeth from the differing ways she speaks to Duncan and Macbeth?' using the ideas above.

> Well, my husband is a very ambitious man, but frankly he is gutless ...

ALERT The best way to understand how a person behaves is AL
to get inside his or her skin.

Romeo and Juliet

Imagine you are Romeo and have just come away from meeting Juliet at the masked ball. Answer the following questions:

- Why did you go to the ball in any case? You are supposed to be in love with Rosaline.
- How did Lord Capulet react to having you, one of his family's sworn enemies, at his celebration?
- What were your feelings when you first saw Juliet?
- What happened when the two of you first met?
- What were your feelings when you realised you had fallen for a Capulet?
- What are you going to do now?

Now look at the question actually set on that scene: 'How does Shakespeare make this scene interesting and tense for his audience?' and consider and see how valuable the hotseating exercise has been.

Remember, when working on or studying a new play, it is always useful to make notes about the main characters – and these notes can be extended and given greater depth by hotseating.

Exercise 2

Twelfth Night

Sir Toby drops a letter for Malvolio to read which will make him think Olivia loves him.
You are Sir Toby.
- Why do you not like Malvolio?
- How do you react when Malvolio says he thinks Olivia loves him?
- What does Malvolio think of you?
- What have you written in the letter?
- Why does it not just say, 'I love Malvolio, signed Olivia'?
- How does Malvolio react to the letter?
- What do you want to happen as a result of Malvolio believing the letter is real?

Answer this question on the scene: 'What advice would you give to your actors to make this scene funny for the audience?'

RED ALERT RED ALERT RED ALERT RED

Presenting a poem

Read this extract:

Romeo:	If I profane with my unworthiest hand
	This holy shrine, the gentle sin is this,
	My lips, two blushing pilgrims, ready stand
	To smooth that rough touch with a tender kiss.
Juliet:	Good pilgrim, you do wrong your hand too
	much,
	Which mannerly devotion shows in this,
	For saints have hands that holy pilgrims' hands
	do touch,
	And palm to palm is holy palmers' kiss.
Romeo:	Have not saints lips, and holy palmers too?
Juliet:	Ay, pilgrim, lips they must use in prayer.
Romeo:	Oh then, dear saint, let lips do what hands do:
	Then pray, grant thou, lest faith turn to despair.
Juliet:	Saints do not move, though grant for prayers' sake.
Romeo:	Then move not while my prayer's effect I take.
(Kissing her)	

These are the first words that Romeo and Juliet exchange. It is a beautiful meeting in which they fall in love at first sight. Shakespeare handles the strength of their emotions brilliantly by writing their opening words in the form of a sonnet – a love poem. A Shakespeare sonnet has 14 lines with a particular rhyming scheme that ends with a rhyming couplet to round

Exercise 1

Make a tape-recording of the speech above – complete with sound effects.

Exercise 2

Do the same speeches in modern English, and tape record them with sound effects.

ALERT The best way of understanding a poem is to hear it read by the poet who wrote it – if that is possible! **AL**

everything off neatly. The characters show they are in harmony by the way in which they create the poem. See how Juliet picks up the way Romeo has delivered the first four lines and replies with words in an identical form. They share the rhyme and end together – with a kiss!

The language is rather hard to understand, but basically what Romeo is saying is that he wants to worship Juliet like a pilgrim and to kiss her. Juliet replies that she is a saint and is happy to touch his hand. Romeo insists on a kiss; Juliet says a saint will not move if he does. So he kisses her. Two lines later, she returns the compliment!

Although this is an excerpt from a play, it is a self-contained poem which two people can share with other by reading it aloud – though you might have to save the kiss for later!

Preparing a paired poetry reading

- Select your poem – one in which there are two voices or two points of view is ideal.
- Discuss it fully so that you understand every word that you will speak.
- See where it divides naturally to allow a change of voice. A new verse is probably the best place but look at the punctuation and at least wait for a full stop.
- Consider how you can vary the speed and volume of delivery for maximum effect.
- Do not be afraid to select parts where you can both speak at the same time.
- Remember your audience might need an introduction.

Exercise 3

Prepare this poem to read aloud.

Woodman, spare that tree

Woodman, spare that tree!
Touch not a single bough!
In youth it sheltered me,
And I'll protect it now.
'Twas my forefather's hand
That placed it near his cot;
There, woodman, let it stand,
Thy axe shall harm it not!

That old familiar tree,
Whose glory and renown
Are spread o'er land and sea –
And wouldst thou hew it down?
Woodman, forbear thy stroke!

Cut not its earth-bound ties;
Oh, spare that aged oak

Now towering to the skies!
My heart-strings round thee cling
Close as thy bark, old friend!
There shall the wild-bird sing,
And still thy branches bend.
Old tree! The storm still brave!
Then, woodman, leave the spot;
While I've a hand to save,
Thy axe shall harm it not!
George Pope Morris
(1802–1864)

Formal activities

The debate

The old-fashioned debate is still one of the most enjoyable ways of discussing an issue. First you need a motion. This is a statement that starts: 'This house ...' and goes on to say something that is open to argument. For example, *This house believes capital punishment is wrong; This school thinks school uniform is great; This house loves beefburgers...*

Now you need five speakers:

- A chairperson: someone who can keep control of the debate, introduce speakers in the correct order, take questions from the floor and conduct the final vote.
- A proposer of the motion: a good speaker who can lay out the arguments for voting in favour of the motion, and who can sum up the arguments in a closing speech.
- A second speaker for the proposer: a good speaker who can supply other good reasons for voting in favour of the motion.
- An opposer of the motion.
- A second speaker for the opposer.

Next agree on the format of the debate:

- Chairperson introduces the speakers;
- The Proposer's speech;

Exercise 1

Imagine you are in a debating team and you are in the finals of a debating competition. In the first debate you are the proposer. Make notes about what you might say. Remember to keep the points salient and concise, and try to consider any counter-arguments you might meet – it can help to have a quick response!

Write notes on these motions:

- This house believes that spelling should be reformed.
- This house thinks things are bad and getting worse.
- This house would abolish Christmas.
- This house hates school.

> Mr Chairman, Ladies and Gentlemen. Sat in room – wondering why anyone hates school – what is there to hate about it? [pause for laughter]

- The Opposer's speech;
- Proposer's second;
- Opposer's second;
- Speeches from the floor;
- Opposer's summing-up;
- Proposer's summing-up;
- Vote.

The key thing is that debates are not meant to be personal slanging matches. They are modelled on what happens in Parliament (and we all know how well-behaved they are!). To keep things impersonal and formal, you should never call anyone else by name – only the chairperson has this right. So you have to refer to 'The proposer of the motion' even though she is called Brenda!

Public speaking competitions

A number of charitable bodies encourage public speaking amongst young people and organise national competitions to foster their talents. Most of these competitions look for teams of three speakers:

- A chairperson to introduce the main speaker;
- The main speaker talking about a subject which is felt strongly;
- A third speaker to express the thanks of the meeting to the main speaker.

One national competition takes a slightly different approach: the chairperson and the main speaker stay together and the third speaker has to give a vote of thanks to a speaker in another team for a speech which s/he has only just heard.

Exercise 2

Speaking clearly is a matter of opening your mouth and working hard to ensure that every vowel and consonant is carefully pronounced. See how quickly and often you can repeat these example of tongue-twisters:

1   Peter Piper picked a peck of pickled peppers.

2   The Leith police dismisseth us.

3   She sells seashells on the seashore.

4   Truly rural.

5   'Whereat, with blade, with bloody blameful blade,
     He bravely broached his boiling bloody breast…'
     A Midsummer Night's Dream

Giving a talk

The favourite activity in oral work is giving a talk about a subject that interests you. Everybody has different enthusiasms and everybody wants to hear what lights up your life but it is not easy to be successful.

Planning your talk on a summer holiday

- Collect together as much information as possible on your subject: photos, posters, leaflets, maps, diagrams, products, postcards and so on.
- Select only that material which can be seen easily from the back of the class. If you want to show a map of where you went, you may need to draw it out on a large sheet of paper.
- Decide which aspect of your holiday you are going to focus upon. You will have done so much that you might just concentrate on a visit you made to a theme park or a site of historical interest.
- Write out your talk in full: you can reckon that the average person speaks about 100 words a minute so for a ten-minute talk, you will want 1,000 words.
- Learn the speech and put it into note-form, like prompts on a postcard which you can hold in one hand and which easily keeps you on track.

Giving the talk

- Make sure that you and what you are wearing are clean and tidy. There is nothing worse than standing in front of an audience and hearing them snigger because your shoes are covered in mud.

Exercise 1

The balloon debate is an excellent game for oral work. In it, the participants have to argue why they should not be thrown out of a balloon which is dangerously losing height. Try these groups:

1   Shakespeare, Prince Charles, The Pope, Margaret Thatcher and Eminem.

2   A chef, a doctor, a teacher, a traffic warden and a Page 3 model.

3   A footballer, a cricketer, an athlete, a tennis player and a boxer.

4   A bus, a car, a motorbike, a scooter and a skateboard.

5   A computer, a mobile phone, a television set and a DVD player.

- Keep still and steady on your feet. You want your audience to listen to you and not be distracted by you hopping up and down on one foot or waving your arms about aimlessly.
- Look at your audience. If it is too embarrassing to look directly at people, direct your eyes to a point in the space in the middle of the back row.
- Open your mouth and speak loudly. There is nothing more irritating than a speaker mumbling away to him or herself.
- Use your notes. A quick look downwards at the notes reassures the audience that you know what you are saying. If you read the whole speech from a paper, the audience quickly becomes bored.
- Make sure that everything you want to show your audience can be seen easily. If you have smaller items, they can be passed around when you have finished.
- Smile at your audience.

These things take practice. You will not be a great speaker first time you stand up – no one ever was. Remember that everyone enjoys listening to other people so they are all on your side. They do not want you to stutter your way through the speech, and you will get a loud round of applause when you succeed.

In the outside world, the ability to give a talk is highly valued wherever you go. The confidence to stand up before a group of your friends comes quite quickly. Being able to go on and talk to a crowd of strangers comes directly from the early encounters with people who know and like you. Go for it!

Exercise 2

Summarise what you think are the three most important things to remember in speaking to an audience.

81

RED   **Never be afraid to inject humour into your speeches.**   **RED**

TEST PAPER 1

The Examination Paper has the following instructions on the front page:

Please read this page, but do not open the booklet until your teacher tells you to start.

Write your name and school on the front of your answer booklet. If you have been given a pupil number, write that also.

• Check your work carefully.

• Ask your teacher if you are not sure what to do.

Section A

Read the following passage. Then answer question 1 and question 2.

The writer of the passage, H G Wells, imagines that his Time-Traveller goes forward in distant time and sees a dying sun shining dimly on a dying earth.

Looking round me again, I saw that, quite near, what I had taken to be a reddish mass of rock was moving slowly towards me. And then I saw the thing was really a monstrous crab-like creature. Can you imagine a crab as large as yonder table, with its many legs moving, slowly and uncertainly, its big claws swaying, its long antennae, like carters' whips, waving and feeling, and its stalked eyes gleaming at you on either side of its metallic front? Its back was corrugated and ornamented with ungainly bosses[1], and a greenish incrustation blotched here and there. I could see the many palps of its complicated mouth flickering and feeling as it moved.

As I stared at this sinister apparition crawling towards me, I felt a tickling on my cheek as though a fly had lighted there. I tried to brush it away with my hand, but in a moment it returned, and almost immediately came another by my ear. I struck at this, and caught something threadlike. It was drawn swiftly out of my hand. With a frightful qualm[2], I turned, and saw that I had grasped the antenna of another monster crab that stood just behind me. Its evil eyes were wriggling on their stalks, its mouth was all alive with appetite, and its vast ungainly claws, smeared with algal slime, were descending upon me.

In a moment my hand was on the lever, and I had placed a month between myself and these monsters. But I was still on the same beach, and I saw them distinctly now as soon as I stopped. Dozens of them seemed to be crawling here and there, in the sombre light, among the foliated³ sheets of intense green.

I cannot convey the sense of abominable desolation that hung over the world. The red eastern sky, the northward blackness, the salt dead sea, the stony beach crawling with these foul, slow-stirring monsters, the uniform poisonous-looking green of the lichenous plants, the thin air that hurts one's lungs; all contribute to an appalling effect. I

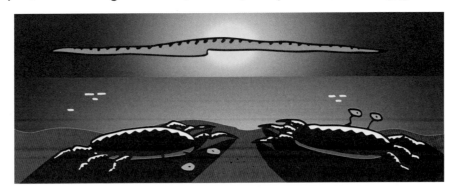

moved on a hundred years, and there was the same red sun – a little larger, a little duller – the same dying sea, the same chill air, and the same crowd of earthy crustacea creeping in and out among the green weed and the red rocks. And in the westward sky I saw a curved pale line like a vast new moon.

From The Time Machine *by H G Wells*

¹bosses – raised lumps   ²qualm – feeling of fear   ³foliated – in layers

Answer question 1 and question 2.

1   Read the first two paragraphs again. How does H G Wells suggest the growing feeling of disgust in these paragraphs? Comment on:
   • how he gradually becomes aware of the threat of the 'crab-like' creatures;
   • how the words he uses and their associations create a growing atmosphere of horror.

Look again at the two expressions below and suggest how they add to the feeling of revulsion.

Evil eyes ... wriggling on their stalks.   *Its mouth ... all alive with appetite.*

(11 marks)

2   Read the final paragraph again. In this paragraph Wells writes: *I cannot convey the sense of abominable desolation that hung over the world.* In fact he **does** *convey desolation* here. Show how he achieves this.

(6 marks)

Section B

Read the passage opposite and then answer question 3 below.
Refer to words and phrases used in the passage to support your ideas.

3   Suggest how Orwell introduces a sense of threat and despair in this passage. In your answer you should comment on:
   • the odd references which alert the reader to question what is going on;
   • the picture we get of Winston Smith;
   • the contrast between the ordinary and the unusual.

(11 marks)

It was a bright cold day in April, and the clocks were striking thirteen. Winston Smith, his chin nuzzled into his breast in an effort to escape the vile wind, slipped quickly through the glass doors of Victory Mansions, though not quickly enough to prevent a swirl of gritty dust from entering along with him.

The hallway smelled of boiled cabbage and old rag mats. At one end of it a coloured poster, too large for indoor display, had been tacked to the wall. It depicted simply an enormous face, more than a metre wide; the face of a man of about forty-five, with a heavy black moustache and ruggedly handsome features... The flat was seven flights up, and Winston, who was thirty-nine and had a varicose ulcer above his right ankle, went slowly, resting several times on the way. On each landing, opposite the lift shaft, the poster with the enormous face gazed from the wall. It was one of those pictures which are so contrived that the eyes follow you about as you move. BIG BROTHER IS WATCHING YOU, the caption beneath it ran.

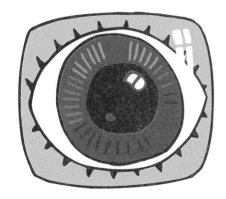

Inside the flat a fruity voice was reading out a list of figures which had something to do with the production of pig iron. The voice came from an oblong metal plaque like a dulled mirror which formed part of the surface of the right-hand wall. Winston turned a switch and the voice sank somewhat, though the words were still distinguishable. The instrument (the tele-screen, it was called) could be dimmed, but there was no way of shutting it off completely... The telescreen received and transmitted simultaneously. Any sound that Winston made, above the level of a very low whisper, would be picked up by it; moreover, so long as he remained within the field of vision which the metal plaque commanded, he could be seen as well as heard. There was no way of knowing whether you were being watched at any given moment.

From 1984 by George Orwell

Shakespeare paper 1

Background

William Shakespeare (1564–1616). Little is actually known for certain about Shakespeare's life. He was born at Stratford-upon-Avon in Warwickshire in 1564. His father has been variously described as a yeoman, a glove maker, a butcher and a wool trader. All that is

known for certain is that Shakespeare's father was of some standing in local life. It is believed that Shakespeare was educated at the free grammar school in Stratford.

He married Anne Hathaway in 1582. They had three children – Susannah and the twins, Judith and Hamnet. Shakespeare left Stratford in about 1585. He is next heard of in London where he became acquainted with the theatre troupes and was given sponsorship by the Earl of Southampton. Although, initially he acted in some plays himself, it is clear that he ceased to be involved as an actor after he became absorbed in writing his plays. He finally 'retired' to Stratford in 1611.

His output was prodigious and he wrote the plays under great pressure.

Useful words: *scene, acquainted, soliloquy, twelfth, character, chorus, prologue.*

Shakespeare was very much a 'popular' playwright of his time.

The theatre itself was considered to be somewhat disreputable and no females were allowed to perform of the stage in this country until after the restoration of the monarchy under Charles II in 1660. Therefore, such characters as Lady Macbeth, Viola, Cleopatra and Juliet were played on the stage by boys.

Shakespeare based the plots of his plays on much that had been written before. 'Originality', as we see it, was not considered an essential. However, it is very interesting to see what Shakespeare and his fellow playwrights did with the material that they re-worked.

Apart from the scenes you will study in detail, you should have a working knowledge of the plot of the play so that you can place the scene you have studied in its context (this means its 'setting').

Shakespeare's plays can be conveniently divided into Histories, Comedies and Tragedies. A History play presented a certain view of historical events and was not necessarily 'true' as we would, perhaps, expect from a documentary today. *Henry V* extols the character and achievements of King Henry as seen from an Elizabethan viewpoint. A comedy was, generally speaking, a play that ended happily after many complications of mistaken identity, disguise, misplaced devotion and misunderstanding. A tragedy in essence, ended unhappily and concerned itself with the downfall of a hero and/or heroine through the influences of fate and their own misplaced ambitions.

A reference book such as *The Oxford Companion to English Literature*, found in the reference section of most libraries, is invaluable in giving you some detailed back up information you will find useful.

Shakespeare paper 2

You will find the following instructions on the first page: 'Please read this page, but do not open the booklet until your teacher tells you to start.'

Write your name and school on the front cover of your answer booklet. If you have been given a pupil number, write that also.

Remember:

- The test is 1 hour and 15 minutes long.
- You should do ONE task on ONE of the following plays:

Henry V

Macbeth

Twelfth Night

- Your work will be assessed for your knowledge and understanding of the play and the way you express your ideas.

- Check your work carefully

- Ask your teacher if you are not sure what to do.

Choose ONE task (on ONE of the plays).

Henry V

Act II scene ii (whole scene)
'Fore God, his grace is bold ... No King of England, if not King of France.

In this scene we see two important characteristics of the now reformed King Henry.

What do you learn from this scene of Henry's ability and dexterity in dealing with the political situation around him? Before you begin to write you should think about:

- What is said by Exeter, Bedford and Westmoreland before Henry's entrance;
- How Henry traps Scroop, Cambridge and Grey by encouraging their flattery;
- Henry's firmness when he 'turns the tables' on Scroop, Cambridge and Grey.

Read the task again before you begin to write your answer.

Macbeth

Act II scene ii (whole scene)
That which hath made me drunk hath made me bold ... Wake Duncan with thy knocking, I would thou couldst.

At the beginning of this scene, we meet Lady Macbeth while her husband has gone to murder King Duncan. When Macbeth returns, he is extremely disturbed.

What do you learn about Lady Macbeth in this scene and the way in which she takes control of the situation? You might consider:

- What she says about her preparations for the murder;
- The way she reacts to her husband's saying he has heard voices;

- The way she talks to him when she realises he has brought the daggers with them;
- How she takes command by the end of the scene.

Read the task again before you begin your answer.

Twelfth Night

Act IV scene i (whole scene)
Will you make me believe that I am not sent for you? ... O, say so, and so be!

In this scene Sebastian is mistaken for Cesario (Viola) by Feste, Sir Toby, Sir Andrew, Fabian and Olivia. (For the purposes of the play Sebastian, Viola's twin, is identical.) Sebastian is, understandably, confused by the apparent familiarity with which he is greeted.

Suggest what you learn from this scene of:

(a) Feste's insight and self-interest;
(b) Sebastian's gullibility.

Before you begin, you might like to consider the following points:

- Feste's reaction to the behaviour of Sir Toby and friends
- Sebastian's reaction to Olivia's request
- How the audience is drawn into the humour of the situation.

ANSWERS

Answers to exercises

Parts of speech

Exercise 1
1 camel – noun
2 interesting – adjective
3 animals – noun
4 in – preposition
5 unfortunately – adverb
6 it – pronoun
7 was – verb
8 soon – adverb
9 perhaps – adverb
10 next – adjective

Exercise 2
1 noun
2 noun
3 noun
4 pronoun
5 adverb
6 verb
7 connective
8 adjective
9 preposition
10 adverb

Exercise 3
Here are some suggested answers, but yours may differ.
1 He opened the book. (noun)
   Can you book me a flight? (verb)
   He was a book fanatic. (adjective)
2 He fiddled with his tie. (noun)
   Can you tie this knot tighter? (verb)
   She bought him a tie rack. (adjective)
3 They laughed all the way through the film. (noun)
   I'd like to film the movie in Hawaii. (verb)
   The film set was teeming with actors. (adjective)
4 Put the flower in the vase. (noun)
   The trees will flower in spring. (verb)
   She bought a bouquet at the flower shop. (adjective)
5 He hung the picture on the wall. (noun)
   Try to picture the scene. (verb)
   She took the photo to the picture framer's. (adjective)
6 Her face was red from crying. (noun)
   He returned to face the music. (verb)
   She kept the face pack on for an hour. (adjective)

Exercise 4
1 him
2 them
3 They
4 her
5 it

Spelling strategies and rules

Exercise 1
1 false
2 false
3 false
4 true
5 true

Exercise 2
1 received
2 beautiful
3 sincerely
4 trolleys
5 chiefs
6 weird
7 niece
8 totally
9 traveller
10 cherries

Common errors

Exercise 1
1 except
2 drawers
3 further
4 It's
5 past
6 piece
7 quiet
8 stationery
9 their
10 were

Exercise 2

1 dessert
2 immigrant
3 angel
4 descent
5 waist
6 lightning
7 weather
8 quiet
9 guerrilla
10 cue

The apostrophe

1 son's
2 You're
3 Peter's
4 girls'
5 day's
6 Jesus'
7 fish's
8 sheep's
9 Spurs'
10 teacher's

Exercise 2

Only three are needed: mother's friends, fishermen's cottages, cat's bowl.

The roots of English

1 hydrant – pipe from a water main
2 thermometer – instrument for measuring temperature
3 dehydration – the state of having lost water
4 viaduct – bridge, especially for carrying a road or railway across a valley
5 speedometer – instrument for measuring speed

Exercise 2

1 mother
2 yourself
3 father
4 king
5 brother
6 a race
7 sperm
8 grass
9 a person
10 insects

Standard English

Exercise 1
All the statements are true.

Exercise 2

1 false
2 true
3 true
4 false
5 false

Punctuation

Exercise 1
"Can I have a wasp, please?" asked the little lad.

"But we don't sell them," said the pet shop owner. "We sell budgies, canaries, mice and snakes, but no wasps."

"That's funny," said the little lad. "You've got one in the window."

Exercise 2
The dash introduces something unexpected. Beware of overuse since it can easily replace all sorts of other punctuation marks and gives the writing a sloppy feel. Here is an example of how it may be used effectively: There's one thing I cannot stand – surprises!

Paragraphing

Exercise 1
The issue of euthanasia has been much in the news lately. As medicine keeps patients alive longer, people are becoming worried that their suffering might be prolonged.
On the other hand, unscrupulous people may use euthanasia as a way to persuade older people that they should take the easy way out of life.
The unscrupulous people might, however, be using the kind nature of the older person to hasten their ending – and thus rid themselves of the trouble of caring for the patient.

Exercise 2
A – 4th, B – 2nd, C – 1st, D – 3rd

ANSWERS

Figures of speech

Exercise 1
1 personification
2 hyperbole
3 personification
4 personification
5 hyperbole

Exercise 2
1 metaphor
2 alliteration
3 metaphor
4 hyperbole
5 simile
6 personification

Sentence construction

Exercise 1
Here are some suggested answers, but yours may differ.
1 The dog was getting wet in the rain and soon he howled to be let in, but there was no one in to hear him.
2 Beethoven is considered to be a great composer who wrote a wide range of music, but, sadly, he became deaf.
3 The gardener was mowing the lawn when it started to rain, so she put away her tools.

Exercise 2

These are some possible answers
variety, short, connective, young, expression.
truly, further, table, eggs, thanks.

Use of quotations

Exercise 1
Oh Romeo, if only you were Fred Smith!

Exercise 2
It is too rash, too unadvis'd, too sudden;// too like the lightning, which doth cease to be// ere one can say 'It lightens'. Sweet, good-night!// This bud of love, by summer's ripening breath,// May prove a beauteous flower when next we meet.

O, when mine eyes did see Olivia first,// Methought she purg'd the air of pestilence!// That instant was I turn'd into a hart;// and my desires, like fell and cruel hounds,// e'er since pursue me.

Reading in paper 1 (1)

Exercise 1
Here are some suggested answers, but yours may differ.
1 Gives the impression of children trapped in their old-fashioned desks, quite unable to move.
2 The teacher looks at the children with beady, sharp and closed-up eyes.
3 The sound the children make when they answer is more like a noise than words.
4 A comic sight of a large person squashed in to a too-small desk.
5 The boy moves easily and smoothly.

Descriptive writing

Exercise 1
Here are some suggested answers, but yours may differ.
1 We had a tremendous picnic the other day.
2 He told me to leave of the room.
3 I had fantastic feeling when I finished first.
4 Ultimately, we would all like to win the lottery.
5 What a beautiful bouquet the bride carried!

Answers to test papers

The test paper answers are all essays and so there is no 'right' answer. Re-read the extracts and questions and check you have answered them clearly.

JARGON BUSTER

Accent	a way of speaking that indicates the origin and class of a person. A northern accent commonly has flattened vowels in such words as *bath*.
Alliteration	the repetition of the same consonant sound for effect, for example: *Around the rugged rock, the ragged rascal ran.*
Antonym	a word meaning the opposite of another, for example: *happy/sad*
Assonance	the repetition of a vowel sound as in: *The year is dying in the night.*
Ballad	a poem that tells a story
Cliché	a phrase or expression which is overused, for example: *She ran like a house on fire.*
Comedy	a play with a happy ending
Dialect	a particular variety of language dependent on the part of the country from which the speaker comes. For instance, a Devonian might say 'Ur's a proper-looking maid', whilst a Scot might describe the same girl as a 'bonnie lass'.
Dramatic irony	a situation on stage when the audience knows something the characters do not. In *Macbeth*, King Duncan says how lovely Macbeth's castle is; we, however, know that he about to be murdered there.
Figurative language or figures of speech	language which is used for effect and which cannot be understood literally
Formal	speech or writing that is used for serious expression
Homophone	a word which is spelled differently from another but pronounced the same, for example: *A tree has a bough whilst a courtier would bow to his king.*
Homonym	a word that is spelled the same but pronounced differently according to its meaning, such as: A man would *row* a boat but if he was unlucky he might *row* with his wife – about the children!
Hyperbole	a figure of speech in which exaggeration is employed, for example: *I had tons of questions to ask.*
Informal	casual or light-hearted speech
Irony	when one thing is said but another meaning is intended
Literal	meaning word-for-word what is said or written

94

Metaphor	a figure of speech where one thing is compared or identified with another dissimilar thing, for example: *That was a half-baked idea.* The idea is compared to food, half-baked meaning it had not been fully thought-through.
Mnemonic	an aid to memory, such as: *EGDBF – every good boy deserves favour.*
Narrative verse	poetry which tells a story
Narrator	the person who tells the story of a play, novel or poem
Onomatopoeia	a word which imitates the sound of what is being described, such as: *Bang! Crash! Wallop!*
Part of speech	the function of a word in a sentence
Personification	a figure of speech where something not human is given human qualities, for example: *The moon wept silently over our house.*
Poetry	language that is given a rhythm and may be rhymed
Prose	language that is not poetry
Pun	a play on words which look or sound the same, for example: *The parson told the sexton/And the sexton tolled the bell.*
Rhyme	the repetition of a similar or identical sound either within or at the end of a line of poetry
Simile	an image that makes a comparison by saying that one thing is like another, such as: *He ran like the wind.*
Standard English	the ideal of language spoken and used by 'educated' users of the language
Sonnet	a fourteen-line poem with a complicated rhyming scheme, originally used to express feelings of love
Stanza	an individual verse in a poem
Syllable	one of the sections a word can be broken down into. *Dog* is a monosyllable, whilst *puppy* has two, *pup* and *py*.
Synonym	a word that has a similar meaning to another. *Happy* and *joyful* are synonymous.
Theme	the subject or subjects covered by a writer, not just the story. *Romeo and Juliet* tells the story of a tragic love affair but its theme concerns the tragedy of love in a divided society.
Tragedy	a play that traces the downfall of a person who suffers from a personality fault. Macbeth ultimately dies because he is blinded by his own ambition.

INDEX

accent 21
argumentative writing 64–65
apostrophe 14–15, 19

bias 45
brainstorming 54

context 46, 53

debates 78–79
descriptive writing 62–63
dialect 21
diaries 69
drafting 54–54

errors, common 12–13, 19
examination, preparation for 72–73

fact and fiction 63
fact and opinion 45, 53
figures of speech 26–27, 33
forms of poetry 41
forms of writing 44–45, 58

genre 53

haiku 57

iambic pentameter 47
imaginative writing 60–61

letters 68

narrative writing 60
newspaper articles 42–43
non-fiction 38–39, 50–51

paragraphs 22–23, 32
parts of speech 6–9, 18
persuasive texts 36–37
persuasive writing 64–65
planning 54–55, 60–61
plot 60–61
poem, presenting a 76–77
poetry, studying 40–41
poetry, writing 56–57
punctuation 24–25, 33
quotations, use of 30–31, 33

reading checklist 52–53
reading strategies 34–35
research 44–45, 65–66
rhyme scheme 41
roots, word 16–17, 19

script, writing a 58
sentence construction 28–29, 33
setting 53
Shakespeare, reading 46–47
spelling 10–11, 18
Standard English 20–21, 32

talk, giving a 80–81

word roots 16–17, 19
writing checklist 70–71
writing poetry 56–57